THE ART OF

THE TALE OF
THE PRINCESS KAGUYA

A FILM BY ISAO TAKAHATA

Cover illustration: S17-C118 key animation/Ei Inoue, Kenichi Koni-
shi. Key animations used in this book colored by Kazuo Oga.
Cover: S17-C118 key animation/Ei Inoue, Kenichi Konishi.
P2–3: S11-C16 background/Kazuo Oga.
P4–5: S3E-C01 background/Kazuo Oga.
P6–7: S17-C109 background/Kazuo Oga.

Contents

About This Book

This collection is made up of character sketches, designs, key animations (including revisions), layouts, concept sketches, backgrounds, and film stills for and from the animated film *The Tale of the Princess Kaguya*. The relevant shot numbers and artist credits are noted for the key animations and backgrounds, with a shot number such as "S5-C123" means "scene 5, sequence 123."

A Few Notes on Cinematic Expression in *The Tale of the Princess Kaguya*

Creator, Screenplay, Director

Isao Takahata

An appreciation

We were in the middle of mixing down the music, watching the big screen at Toho Studios, when musician Joe Hisaishi whispered to me, "Every flame is worthy of being its own painting."

I was so happy. I went back to the studio and immediately told the staff.

This accomplishment was akin to a miracle. I had acquired the wonderful talents of Kazuo Oga and Osamu Tanabe right at the start of the filmmaking process, but I worried that fusing their two idiosyncratic art styles while also maintaining their distinctive impacts for the entirety of a feature-length animated film—made by dividing labor into a range of processes—might prove impossible. These two artists showed off not only their talent but their astounding work ethic as they drew a truly vast number of images. I am delighted that I was able to produce such a film with the likes of Oga and Tanabe. I also want to express my immense respect for and gratitude to the entire crew, who worked unceasingly to maintain the quality of these images, sparing absolutely no effort—from supervising animator Kenichi Konishi and all the excellent animators representing the best of Japan to the photography team taking care of the final processes and everyone involved in the production. If it hadn't been for their talent, creativity, and devotion, this film would never have seen the light of day. Thank you.

Keyword: Sketch

Every flame is worthy of being its own painting, characters and backgrounds perfectly unified—this was for us a very happy assessment. In this book, you will be able to see some of the secrets behind how this was accomplished. But no matter how marvelous the images that appear on-screen they cannot be anything if they don't make themselves lively as a visual expression of cinema. I am confident that they are indeed alive in that way. I did a number of interviews after we finished the film and tried to talk about exactly this, but I wasn't able to explain very well. I can, however, sum up why this film is alive in terms of cinematic expression, and why it has power to appeal to people: essentially, our expression is the sketch itself via line drawings.

I recently happened upon an art criticism by the eighteenth-century Enlightenment thinker and *Encyclopédie* contributor Denis Diderot alluding to the appeal of the *esquisse* (French for "sketch"). His words resonated deeply with me, and they also hit upon the secret to the power of our own visual expression, so allow me to quote some of them here:

"Why do we prefer a beautiful esquisse to a beautiful tableau? Because it has more life and less form. As it moves toward form, it loses life. [...] The reason that the sketch captures our attention so powerfully is because it leaves our creativity a greater freedom in that it is undefined, so our creativity allows us to see everything we like in it."

"We prefer the esquisse to the tableau because we feel the possibilities trembling within it."

"There is a fire in the esquisse that is not normally in the tableau. This is the time of the artist's passion. [...] It is the soul of the painting that spreads out as it will on the canvas."

"The esquisse is a product of passion and genius, while the tableau is a product of work, of perseverance, of long practice, and of mature experience."

An esquisse is a lively depiction in which the artist tries to capture their subject in a particular moment: the tension and passion of an act not yet complete, the artless beating of the heart when facing the subject. This freshness calls to the heart of the viewer to imagine what else is involved with the object, its depths; to search their memories, to actively understand, to feel the feelings the sketch calls up.

The lines, washes, and blank spaces in the animated film *The Tale of the Princess Kaguya* were an attempt to bring about this exact "lively depiction." Of course, our depiction was completely different from your average sketch. It was, in fact, the product "of work, of perseverance, of long practice" by many people. And yet we had to somehow imbue it with that original "passion and genius" because otherwise, the freshness would not reach the viewers. And given that we were making a movie, this power had to be maintained over time. In order to achieve this contradictory and difficult task in each and every shot, it was essential that we experiment over and over with every detail. The creation of the work thus became a thrilling adventure of sorts.

Tanabe's character modeling isn't a matter of simply checking the boxes on a list of character traits, nor is it derived from a minor detail based on actual people. Rather, it is the lively depiction in linework, scooping up the idiosyncrasies, impressions, and reality of each moment. He makes these characters move in a real way and captures that movement on the page. He draws small, then blows the drawings up. Through breaks and differentiated line weights, he imbues his linework with qualities of "trembling" and force. He leaves parts unpainted, just dabs a bit of color in. He takes risks, sometimes putting more uncolored spaces on the page, sometimes fewer, sometimes making the lines more shaky, sometimes less. All these tricks that Tanabe led us to were to maintain the "passion and genius" Diderot spoke of, to have the artist's fresh beating heart capture the viewer, spark imagination, and call up memories.

If we read the third Diderot quote as being about rough frames and final films instead of esquisses and tableaux, we could easily say it applies to the expression we see in the scene where Princess Kaguya is racing away (animated by Shinji Hashimoto), in which passion is most certainly communicated to the viewer.

To fix a sketch in memory, one must depict the desired subject quickly, capturing it in the bare minimum of line and color. With this objective, one must either simplify those things known from daily life or not draw them at all. It's only natural that some things would be left out, unpainted. I don't speak only about characters; it's the same for backgrounds. Just because there is night or the sky, one doesn't need to paint everything black or blue.

However, in the case of *The Tale of the Princess Kaguya*, a major theme of the work is the diverse richness of nature; thus, an appealing depiction of nature is essential. I wanted to do this not by locking people up in a realistic trompe l'oeil version of nature, but by stirring their imaginations and calling up their best memories. I wanted people to play in nature, fondly and warmly. To that end, skilled pencil and wash drawings alone were not enough; I needed that freshness of the sketch. Although our depiction frequently reached for subtle details, we still captured the freshness roughly, casually, in sketch-like brushwork; tossed some color in; and left the white loosely from the paper, allowing a comfortable breeze to blow through. The only person who could manage something like this is Oga, and this is the artistic expression he led us to.

Sketching could already be seen as early as the twelfth century in Japan in picture scrolls such as *Chōjū Giga*, *Shigisan Engi Emaki*, *Ban Dainagon Ekotoba*, and *Nenchu Gyoji Emaki*. Travellers in the Edo period left behind many sketches done with portable inks and brushes.

Dynamic natural phenomena such as flowing water, waves, flames, smoke, lightning, and even the rotating wheels of vehicles have been expressed in linework in Japan since the long-ago twelfth century. The artists made abstract the irregular shapes that were difficult to capture and created an image of how the scene looked to them personally (while referring to techniques imported from China). The smoke puffs up, the waves shimmer, vehicles trundle along. I believe it was because they keenly felt the energy of the whole of creation that they felt compelled to express it. It's quite unfortunate that, with the development of computer graphics, this tradition is disappearing.

Ever since *My Neighbors the Yamadas*, out of love for the art, we have tried to raise questions about the tendency in Japanese animated films toward CG and baroque expression

such as solid bodies, shading, and exaggeration. *The Tale of the Princess Kaguya* is another stone thrown in that direction.

Isao Takahata: Director of animated films. Born October 1935. Graduated from the University of Tokyo with a degree in French literature in 1959. In college, he saw the feature-length animated film *La Bergère et le Ramoneur* (1952; revised and released in 1979 as *Le Roi et l'Oiseau*), discovered the possibilities of animation as a means of expression, and started working at Toei Doga (now Toei Animation) that same year. After working as an assistant director on *The Little Prince and the Eight-Headed Dragon*, he directed the TV series *Wolf Boy Ken* (1963–65). He directed his first feature length film, *The Great Adventure of Horus, Prince of the Sun*, in 1968, and during that time, he deepened his communication with the younger Hayao Miyazaki through their work and union activities. In 1971, he moved to A Production (now Shin-Ei Animation), and then to Zuiyo Enterprise in 1973, where he directed all episodes of *Heidi, Girl of the Alps* (1974). At Nippon Animation, he directed *3000 Leagues in Search of Mother* (1976) and *Anne of Green Gables* (1979). After that, he directed the films *Downtown Story* (1981) and *Gauche the Cellist* (1982). He worked as a producer on *Nausicaä of the Valley of the Wind* (1984) and *Castle in the Sky* (1986). He wrote and directed the films *Grave of the Fireflies* (1988), *Only Yesterday* (1991), *Pom Poko* (1994), and *My Neighbors the Yamadas* (1999). Additionally, he directed the feature-length documentary *The Story of Yanagawa's Canals* in 1987. He also translated and produced the Japanese version of *Kirikou and the Sorceress* (2003) and translated the Japanese subtitles for *Le Roi et l'Oiseau* (2006). He also had a hand in translating and producing the Japanese version of *Azur & Asmar: The Princes' Quest* (2007).

During this time, while he lectured in the Nihon University College of Art film department, he was busy writing a number of works. In *Juni Seiki no Animation* (Tokuma Shoten), he argued that the picture scrolls from the end of the Heian period, which are national treasures, are very much like cinematic animation, and he did the first translation into Japanese of the French poet Jacques Prévert's *Paroles* (Pia). In this way, he was very active as an author. In 1998, he was awarded a purple Medal of Honor. In 2009, he won the Golden Leopard at the Locarno Film Festival, and in 2010, he won a Tokyo Anime Award. *The Tale of the Princess Kaguya* (2013) achieved much international success, including a nomination for the Academy Award for Best Animated Feature in 2015. Takahata passed away on April 3, 2018.

From Conception to Completion

The Tale of the Princess Kaguya is the nineteenth feature-length animated film from Studio Ghibli, released by director Isao Takahata fourteen years after his film *My Neighbors the Yamadas* (1999). After *My Neighbors the Yamadas*, Takahata considered several projects for his next film. *The Tale of the Heike* was one of the stronger candidates, but for a number of reasons, the project didn't make any headway. At the beginning of 2005, producer Toshio Suzuki came to him with *The Tale of the Bamboo Cutter* because he remembered Takahata talking for some time about how this story should be made into a movie someday.

While it's unknown who wrote *The Tale of the Bamboo Cutter* or when, it is the oldest story in Japan, known as a children's tale to all Japanese people.

For Takahata's first encounter with this ancient story, we have to go back in time to a moment not long after he started working at Toei Doga (now Toei Animation). Fifty-five years ago, live-action Toei director Tomu Uchida (whose major works include *Swords in the Moonlight* and the five-part *Miyamoto Musashi*) was working on a project to create a *The Tale of the Bamboo Cutter* animation and had solicited treatments (concise summaries of a plot) from all employees. At first, Takahata wasn't particularly interested in the story, but while considering the question of why exactly Princess Kaguya comes to Earth, he gradually became more and more curious about this classic tale. He came up with the idea that something had happened on the moon, and that she'd come to Earth as a result. In the end, Toei Doga didn't proceed with the project, but Takahata felt that an animated adaptation of *The Tale of the Bamboo Cutter* could be interesting, and he began thinking that someday a Japanese person ought to properly make it into a film.

At the time, he couldn't simply declare himself its director, so he moved forward on the project with a young producer. However, they were unable to make it happen, and at the end of 2005, this project to make *The Tale of the Bamboo Cutter* into an animation disappeared.

Toshio Suzuki then proposed an adaptation of Shugoro Yamamoto's *Yanagibashi Monogatari* (Yanagibashi story), which is set at the end of the Edo era. After reading the novel, Osamu Tanabe drew a number of character sketches, but Takahata couldn't make a feature film with those images. He said he had no intention of doing *Yanagibashi Monogatari*, and instead, he suggested a project based on *Komoriuta no Tanjo* (Birth of a Lullaby) by Norio Akasaka.

Komoriuta no Tanjo is an academic work about the lullabies sung by the lullaby girls who once existed in Japan, but Takahata thought he could take this book as a subject, expand on the idea, create scenes, build a story, and turn it into a movie. He started to work on *Komoriuta no Tanjo* in February 2007, but because he was only able to put together a few scenes that didn't solidify into a framework for a film, the project was shelved.

In spring 2008, Takahata turned once more to *The Tale of the Bamboo Cutter* and started the work of turning *The Tale of the Princess Kaguya* into a film.

But just as had happened the first time, he was unable to produce anything concrete. At the suggestion of Yoshiaki Nishimura, who had been a part of the project since eyes were on *Yanagibashi Monogatari*, they decided to first go ahead with producing a script. The screenwriter finished a first draft in February 2009, but because the content largely differed from the direction Takahata intended, it was decided that Takahata himself would write the script. When he had trouble making headway with it, he looked into getting another screenwriter. In July, he watched the NHK TV drama *Oshasha no Shan!* and was impressed, so he asked the writer of the show, Riko Sakaguchi, to join the project. On August 9, she submitted a nineteen-page synopsis. Takahata approved the synopsis, and Sakaguchi started writing the script.

On September 29, a preparation room was set up on the floor of Studio No. 1, the same studio as *The Secret World of Arrietty*, directed by Hiromasa Yonebayashi, which was in the middle of production at the time, and the short film *Mr. Dough and the Egg Princess*, directed for Ghibli Museum by Hayao Miyazaki. The first draft of the script, finished on October 20, was three and a half hours long. Takahata, Sakaguchi, and Nishimura cut it down to two and a half hours and got the provisional script together. Upon reading the provisional script, producer Suzuki decided to officially make it at Studio Ghibli after a discussion with Hayao Miyazaki.

Supervising animator Kenichi Konishi and animator Miwa Sasaki then joined the project, and the team got to work on creating the film's look.. For the art, Takahata wanted Kazuo Oga, the art director on films like *My Neighbor Totoro* and *Only Yesterday*, but Oga hadn't accepted an art director position in the decade since *Princess Mononoke*, so these negotiations were difficult. Producer Nishimura temporarily put a hold on their attempts to persuade him to take the job.

Going into 2010, Osamu Tanabe made progress drawing the storyboard with Isao Takahata, and while they worked on that, Riko Sakaguchi came back to tweak the script, which she finished on April 16. In June of the same year, Takahata and Nishimura visited Oga, who had finished work on *The Secret World of Arrietty*, and asked him once again to take the position of art director. This time, Oga accepted. On June 12, the main staff moved away from the preparation room in Studio No. 1 and into a studio specially prepared for Princess Kaguya —"Studio Kaguya"—where they started to prepare for the actual production.

In September 2010, animators joined the team and production started on animatics. In October, the animatics were complete. Animation production began at the beginning of 2011. Shinji Hashimoto and Takayuki Hamada came on board as animators. The production of a pilot film was then settled on through an order from Suzuki.

On March 11, 2011, the Tohoku earthquake happened, and some of the staff returned to their hometowns. Studio Kaguya saw periodic rolling blackouts. On March 28, there came the sad news that Seiichiro Ujiie, president of Nippon TV and a longtime supporter of the film, had passed away.

In the middle of all this, work on the storyboards and production on the pilot film continued. In April of that year, the pilot film was completed. A screening was held on April 28.

Yoshiyuki Momose, in charge of the flying scene, then joined the team, along with Shinsaku Sasaki and Masako Sato, who worked on the storyboards.

In August and September of that year, and then again in August 2012, a prescoring script based on the provisional script was used and recording of sound began with voice actors. The prescoring process is the technique and voices of the cast playing the parts before filming, and is an essential process for Takahata films, with the performances of the actors here also used in the later animation work.

As production progressed, the number of people working in each section increased. As a result, in February 2012, production had to move studios once more. The staff continued to focus on the production at the base known as Studio No. 7.

At a press conference on December 13, Studio Ghibli announced the same-day releases of Hayao Miyazaki's *The Wind Rises* and Isao Takahata's *The Tale of the Princess Kaguya* in the summer of 2013. The first poster for *The Tale of Princess Kaguya* was unveiled, and a special promotional video was shown at theaters across the country.

Around this time, the delay in the storyboards became a serious issue on the production frontlines, and the decision was made to focus on storyboard production for the time being. Yoshiyuki Momose, who had been involved in most of Takahata's works up to that point, was asked to do the storyboards for the final sequence. Everyone worked to speed things up.

In January 2013, it was decided that Joe Hisaishi would do the music for a film directed by Takahata for the first time. On February 5, it was announced that the film's release would be delayed to the fall.

On March 23, the storyboard work was completed. On July 29, the layout work was finished, and on August 3, the rough key animation work was done.

On August 19, the official release date of November 23 was announced.

On September 4, the work on key animations was done, and background art was completed on the 7th.

On September 10, the cast came in once more and began recording.

On September 30, the rushes came back; on October 28, the prelim came back; on October 30, there was the first screening; and the movie was released nationwide on November 11.

In the end, there were 1,423 sequences, 237,858 pages of animation, and the final run time was 137 minutes, 17.4 seconds.

Character Design and Animation

The animation for *The Tale of the Princess Kaguya* was drawn by over a hundred animators working on key animations. The animators were led by Osamu Tanabe, who was in charge of character design, and supervising animator Kenichi Konishi. In this section, we hear from Osamu Tanabe on behalf of the animation staff and introduce sketches, key animations, and layouts.

S7-C22 key animation/Kenichi Konishi
Key animation used in the film colored by Kazuo Oga.

Character Design, Directing Animator
Osamu Tanabe

With help from the many members of our staff, I managed to finish the work.

Osamu Tanabe: Born 1965, Okayama prefecture. After graduating with a degree in education from Okayama University, he started work at the animation studio Oh! Production. He worked on the OVA series *The Hakkenden* and the TV special *Like the Clouds, Like the Wind*, among other works, before starting out as a freelancer and working on the theatrical release *Junkers Come Here* (1995) and the TV series *Famous Dog Lassie* (1996). For Studio Ghibli, he was an animator on *Only Yesterday* (1991) and *Pom Poko* (1994). Together with Yoshiyuki Momose, he worked on the storyboards, settings, and animation for *My Neighbors the Yamadas* (1999). In addition to feature-length works, he has also done animation for commercials for Asahi bottled tea (2001), Lawson's *Spirited Away* tickets (2001), Lawson's *Ponyo* tickets (2008), the *Yomiuri Shimbun* (2004/5), and the music video for "Dore Dore no Uta," among many other projects.

Osamu Tanabe worked on *My Neighbors the Yamadas* (1999), directed by Isao Takahata, and was directing animator and in charge of character design for *The Tale of the Princess Kaguya*. Eight years after the project began, the film was completed, thanks to the large staff involved. Tanabe talks to us about how he created the characters and his thoughts behind the design of the animation.

***The Tale of the Princess Kaguya* reached an impasse at one time and turned into a different project before coming back to its starting point. What were you working on when the project was first launched?**
Tanabe: To be honest, I've forgotten the details from the very beginning. I remember Takahata talking to me about maybe creating the characters first.

What did you talk about with Takahata in terms of character design and the overall art style of the film?
Tanabe: I don't think we talked specifically about this or that in particular. At first it was more just draw it and see. After a bit, he said he wanted to make the princess more dignified.

Was there anything you kept in mind while drawing?
Tanabe: This is something I was thinking about before *The Tale of the Princess Kaguya*, but when I would think about what style to draw film characters in, I had a desire to make images that were connected with where I was at that moment. Rather than beautifying or debasing the people around me, I felt it would be great if I could objectively express the different people in equivalent ways.

With a conventional art style, the balance of a single face can look very different, too.
Tanabe: This is also part of capturing them objectively. Even when they're facing slightly forward, I try to be aware of and capture the space between the corner of the eye to the ear. You've got eyes stuck to either side of the human face, surprisingly. I was careful not to make the Japanese eyelids too thick or the chin too short. Looking at the twelfth-century picture scrolls, you can tell that they were drawn with careful attention to these points.

***Princess Kaguya* takes place in the Heian era. Were you then paying attention to the faces of women from that period?**
Tanabe: I wasn't thinking about that at all. The typical image of a Heian beauty is the hooked nose, almond eyes, eyebrows drawn small on the forehead. But Takahata used to often wonder if they were really like that and where exactly that image came from. And while it's true that some of the women in the picture scrolls do have the hooked nose and the almond eyes, if you look at them with that in mind, that's what you'll see. You could also view these as the "artistic model" for the times. The space between the eyes and the eyebrows looks the same in any picture for both nobles and commoners, and the drawn eyebrows are actually surprisingly long.

What about the bamboo cutter and his wife?
Tanabe: Soon after I started drawing the bamboo cutter's wife, I was confident I had to do it not with the idea of a "granny" but of a mom. Takahata didn't have any particular notes when he looked at the pictures I'd drawn. Conversely, even after I had the basic model of the bamboo cutter in my head, it took a while to get it onto the page. And then when we were working on the storyboards, I came to realize that with the face I had been drawing for him, there were limits to the range of emotion. It became apparent that it would be hard to express the emotions needed in the story with the model I initially drew. His mouth, for instance. I did it fairly large, but I couldn't get that expression of "Oh? What's this?" He ended up with this constantly glum look. And with just the round, black eyes, the look of surprise was weaker. This might have been fine for a side character, but the bamboo cutter shows up a lot. I realized that I was too fixated on a very Japanese model and that I wouldn't be able to produce the expressions that Takahata wanted, so I changed his face. I decided not to be too focused on sticking with a set design, to change the design according to the situation.

You abandoned the idea of a granny for the bamboo cutter's wife. In the original story, the bamboo cutter and his wife are around fifty years old, which isn't really that old from our perspective.
Tanabe: That's true. Initially, I was drawing pictures with the bamboo cutter slightly stooped, but one day, Takahata suggested it might be better if he could move a little easier since there is a lot of running in the second half of the film. So the bamboo cutter ended up the way he is now. It was incredibly difficult to draw his proportions. He doesn't stand perfectly upright, his head sticks forward just a bit, and that balance is hard. If his back is too curved or too straight, that changes the sense of his age. It was hard right up until the end. From an animation perspective, people who are middle aged or slightly older are harder to draw. But the difficulty of it is what makes it satisfying.

1, 2/Initial character rough sketches for the princess and Sutemaru drawn by Osamu Tanabe.

Was it difficult for the animators, too?

Tanabe: I guess the bamboo cutter was particularly difficult. Looking at the image I did, I added a slight correction to the curve in his back. In fact, at the stage when the key animation work was beginning, I hadn't set the character designs. While I was doing the layout checks (*1), I decided on the designs with images I added elements to as necessary, like, "Please do the characters who appear in each scene, each shot, like this, thanks." But people said this was too vague and made it hard to draw, so about six months into the animation, I finally set the designs.

Along the lines of "please refer to this when drawing"?

Tanabe: I gave a character sheet to the animators, but they looked at the images and came to me with questions like, "Exactly how tall is this character?" That said, even though I set the designs, during the layout check, it was more like, okay this is the standard, but actually, we changed the character proportions to meet the needs of each sequence. This might have been an extra seed of confusion for the animators.

Compared to your previous work, was the way things were done this time pretty standard?

Tanabe: Not really. It's not entirely uncommon, but that's probably more for animation created by one person or a small number of people.

Takahata films are produced with a prescoring that records the dialogue before the animation. When you have the voices first, how does that affect the animation process?

Tanabe: For *Only Yesterday* (1991), I watched the video of the prescoring recording and referred to that when I was drawing facial expression key frames, but I didn't go that far this time. The recording was two years earlier (August 2011), and there was the script and the character sheet, but since the storyboards were only half-finished, the actors were able to perform how they wished without being too tied to the images. Before meeting with the animators, Takahata listened to the recording and set out the timing for the voices. He places a lot of importance on the spacing between lines, so he would give very detailed instructions, like the timing with the voice now is like this, but leave a little more space here in the dialogue.

Was there anything in the animation that changed because of the prescoring?

Tanabe: We had the animators do the work after listening to the voices. This was at the storyboard stage, and the performances were fairly stylized and put together, so there were few changes. But Takeo Chii gave this very fiery performance as the bamboo cutter, and some images in the board ended up looking a little too subdued. We had already done the key animations for when the bamboo cutter gets all worked up, shouting for the princess, but when we put it together with Chii's voice, the expression we'd drawn seemed too low-key. So I apologized to the animator Takayuki Hamada and had him change it to be more over the top.

The bamboo cutter looks like Chii, but there are also times when he looks like Takahata. Did you have a model for him?

Tanabe: I'd already finished the majority of the character modeling by the time the voice actors were decided on, so they were asked to consider the role with those images in mind. And it's not the case that Takahata was the model for the bamboo cutter. But during production, he gave detailed instructions for each shot, and he would act things out, throw in some gestures

and movement, so it might be that Takahata ended up naturally projected onto him. [*laughs*]

This film was an attempt to have the feel of the pencil lines in the key animations used in the final images. In a normal animated movie, the linework is unified through the entire film by tracing the key animations and drawing changes at the stage of creating the movement, but here, the lively lines of the key animations are reflected almost exactly as they are.

Tanabe: I don't think the style here is special as a technique. In *My Neighbors the Yamadas*, we also incorporated this kind of thing. Since filming went digital, there has been more and more of animation with idiosyncratic linework, like in the animated part of *Kill Bill* (2003) and *Doraemon: Nobita's Dinosaur* (2006).

I'm sure that just as the lines in comics can be thicker or thinner depending on the artist, there must have been differences in the weight of the pencil lines depending on the animator. How did you unify those styles?

Tanabe: Supervising animator Kenichi Konishi really worked hard there. I guess the lines I draw have a certain regularity to them, and Konishi picked up on that and gave detailed instructions on the revision of the finished key animations. At the animating stage, Maiko Nogami, who checked the in-betweens, really scrutinized the lines. She made sure that the weight was unified on each page.

I also felt this during *My Neighbors the Yamadas*, but even if the personality of the person who drew it really comes out when you look at the line drawing, once you add color to that, I feel like there's not that sense of discrepancy when you look at the single image, like it mitigates it. Even if there's variation in the individual key animations, once you add color and set them in motion, a kind of unity does appear.

That's a movie magic particular to animation. What sort of requests did you make of the animators?

Tanabe: Initially, I asked them not to worry about the key animation lines and draw whatever lines were easiest. I thought that if the lines they drew without thinking were good, we could use them. But when they were drawing freely, the feel of the characters changed a lot—if it were a live-action film, it would have been like a new actor took over the role—so for the new animators who joined later, I asked them to please match the detailed nuances of the lines. But depending on the scene, there are also places where we made use of the personality of the key animation. The animator Shinji Hashimoto drew that scene where the princess is running, which was also in the trailer, and he had these incredibly particular drawn-out lines, and I didn't touch those at all. There are a few scenes like that.

But then the work the in-between animation (*2) must have also been rough?

Tanabe: The animation work for this one was really rough. They had to draw every single key animation taking into consideration what was drawn on other pages, like the revised parts of the original art, while bringing to life that art's linework. And to bring out the softness of the kimono, they drew the patterns on each and every page without using CG to match the flow of the fabric. I think the burden to combine these complicated elements into one image was pretty big for Kakita and the other finishers.

Even for in-between animation, a fair bit of skill is required.

Tanabe: When we were doing *My Neighbors the Yamadas*, I had the animators draw everything, including the in-betweens, and I checked the movement with Takahata with the QAR (quick action recorder) (*3). But there were far more lines this time than with *My Neighbors the Yamadas*, so I couldn't actually ask that of the animators. But several of the animators who had worked on *My Neighbors the Yamadas* said, "You do actually want us to do that, though?" and drew everything including the in-between animation for me.

I suppose it was hard on supervising animator Kenichi Konishi, too.
Tanabe: Konishi breathed life into each and every frame, all while respecting my art. The work I draw tends to have a light touch. In particular, I think he gave the princess an intelligent and delicate expression. And when I was overwhelmed with the animation check and the sequences were piling up, Oga from art did the layout for me at a steady pace before I saw the characters. That was really a huge help. The last scene too, where the people from the moon come to get the princess— Momose handled the storyboard and the layout, while Nakamura [Keisuke] patiently photographed the vague and complex elements. If I mentioned everyone, there'd be no end to it, but the staff really did help me out so much, and we were able to finally complete the film.

Notes
1/Layout check
After the animation production meeting, the director and supervising animator examine the layouts drawn by the animators, make corrections to the positions of props and characters, and determine the composition of the screen. For *The Tale of the Princess Kaguya*, this work was mainly carried out by Osamu Tanabe and Kazuo Oga.
2/In-between animation
To show motion within a shot, key movements such as the beginning, middle, and end of the motion are drawn on the key frames, and the process of inserting movement between one key frame and another is called in-betweening. The speed and nuance of the movement change depending on the number of frames.
3/QAR (quick action recorder)
This device loads the key frames and in-betweens, and shows them moving on the screen like a flipbook. This allows the staff to check the movement before photography.

3

4

5

3–5/Imageboard drawn by Osamu Tanabe in the initial stages of production.

Animation Drawing Gallery

Designs, layouts, key animations

This section offers a selection of the vast number of designs, layouts, and key animations drawn in the animation of *The Tale of the Princess Kaguya* and introduces the appeal of the pencil touches that are one of the charms of the film. The comments throughout are from directing animator Osamu Tanabe, who was responsible for character design. For the key animations and layouts, the numbers in square brackets refer to the number of the scene or shot in the film and are noted with the name of the animator who drew the key animation. Images with no name listed were drawn by Osamu Tanabe.

1

Princess Kaguya • Princess, Li'l Bamboo

Born in a bamboo forest, she is raised by an old bamboo cutter and his wife. Given the nickname "Li'l Bamboo" by the children of the mountain, she grows to the age of around thirteen in the span of less than a year.

1/Slightly grown princess. [Character rough sketch]
"The design of the princess's kimono is based on the short-sleeved kimono my wife made when we had a child. Takahata said he wanted to put a scene in somewhere with her wearing a kimono with long, baggy sleeves. I used this kimono design when she starts to walk and meets the wild boar piglets."

About the character design and key animations
The character design here is based on rough sketches drawn by Osamu Tanabe and refined by Osamu Tanabe and Kenichi Konishi. For the frames, when the person doing the roughs and the cleanup are different, both names are noted. Some images also include revisions by supervising animator Kenichi Konishi.

2/Princess trying to roll over. She's putting some effort into it, but her own right hand is in the way and she rolls back down. [S2A-C4 key animation/Takayuki Hamada, Atsushi Tamura]

3/Croaking like the tree frog that has approached her. [S2B-C16 key animation/Takayuki Hamada]

4/Princess crossing her eyes to look at the small spider that has dropped down in front of her. [S2B-C13 key animation/Takayuki Hamada]

5/Princess running around happily. [S2C-C8 key animation/Takayuki Hamada, Tomomi Kamiya]

6/Princess, delighted beyond measure, petting the wild boar piglets who have come over to her. [S2D-C11 key animation/Shoko Nishigaki]

1/Princess at age five. [Character rough sketch]
2/Princess sleeping next to the bamboo cutter's wife. [S3D-C13 key animation/Akiko Yamaguchi]
"Initially, in the rough storyboard that Takahata drew, the princess was sleeping a ways away from the bamboo cutter's wife. But I wanted to portray at least a little physical intimacy in the mountain life, so I discussed it with Takahata, and he made it so that she was sleeping right next to her."
3/Lifting up Hei's little brother to help him pick the low-hanging mountain grapes. [S3E-C12 layout revision]

4

5

4/She quietly sits up, raises her lowered face, opens her eyes, and stares at Inbe no Akita. [S7-C32 key animation/Miwa Sasaki; supervisor revision/Kenichi Konishi]
"This is easily the most close-up shot in the film. Takahata asked for any number of retakes, and we redrew it. After that, supervising animator Konishi got involved and made it even more subtle."
5/Princess around the time she begins life in the capital. [Character design]
"When I was making the character sheet to give out to the animators, Kenichi Konishi helped, mostly with the images of the princess."

1

1/Princess racing down the capital's main avenue. [S7-C80 key animation/Shinji Hashimoto]
2/Four frames of a shot of her falling on the mountain slope. [S7-C84 key animation/Shinji Hashimoto]

3/The wild figure of the princess, ragged and worn. [Character rough sketch]
"At Takahata's suggestion, I left the bamboo branch in the one hand and part of her red hakama trousers as accents."
4/ Collapsed on the snow-covered plain, passed out. [S8-C41 key animation/Kumiko Kawana; supervisor revision/Kenichi Konishi]
"The image I drew during the layout revision was a little dirty, but Konishi enjoyed that dirtiness, and deliberately added touches to her face. I also asked the person doing the finishing to bring out that feeling."

1

1/Hair variations when the princess is sixteen years old.
[Character rough sketch]
2/Princess confessing to the bamboo cutter and his wife
that she must return to the moon. She looks down as she
continues to talk. [S15-C28 key animation/Kuniyuki Ishii]

2

3

3/The bamboo cutter's wife snuggled up to the princess crying in anguish. The princess suddenly looks at her with teary eyes and hugs her. [S15-C15 layout revision]
4/Princess in her moon robes, having forgotten everything about Earth. She heads to the moon, expressionless, but... [S17-C117 key animation/Miwa Sasaki, Kumiko Kawana, Masako Sato]

4

The bamboo cutter

The father who raises Princess Kaguya. His occupation is cutting bamboo. He finds Princess Kaguya while harvesting bamboo and decides to raise her as his daughter.

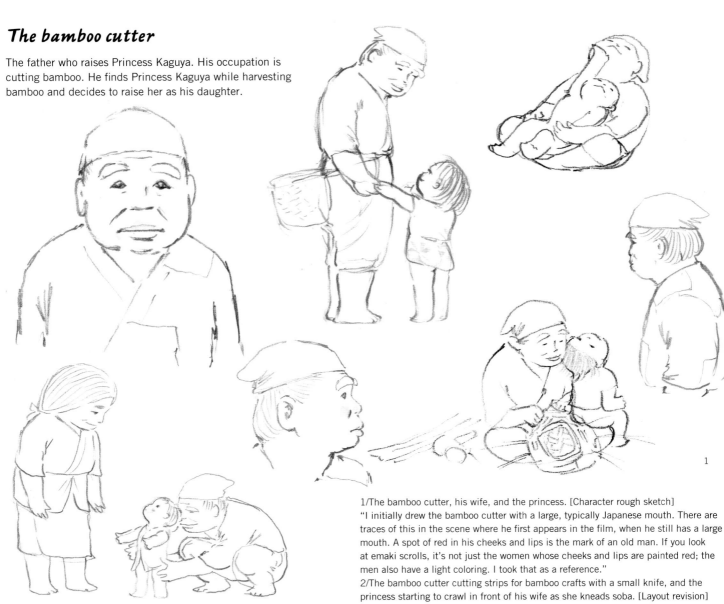

1

1/The bamboo cutter, his wife, and the princess. [Character rough sketch]
"I initially drew the bamboo cutter with a large, typically Japanese mouth. There are traces of this in the scene where he first appears in the film, when he still has a large mouth. A spot of red in his cheeks and lips is the mark of an old man. If you look at emaki scrolls, it's not just the women whose cheeks and lips are painted red; the men also have a light coloring. I took that as a reference."
2/The bamboo cutter cutting strips for bamboo crafts with a small knife, and the princess starting to crawl in front of his wife as she kneads soba. [Layout revision]

2

4

3

6

5

9

8

7

3, 4/Reacting to the bamboo cutter's call, the princess starts walking toward him, and the bamboo cutter is overwhelmed with joy. [S2B-51 revision by supervising animator /Kenichi Konishi]
5–9/The bamboo cutter jumps out into the yard in bare feet, lifts the princess up, and hugs her tightly. [S2B-C52 key animation (5, 6)/Takayuki Hamada, layout revision (7, 8, 9)]
"Hamada, Konishi, and I all have small kids, so our "doting daddy" selves were projected onto the bamboo cutter in this shot. [*laughs*]"

The bamboo cutter's wife

The wife of the bamboo cutter and Princess Kaguya's adoptive mother. She understands the princess's goodness.

1/The bamboo cutter, his wife, and the princess. [Character rough sketch]

2/The bamboo cutter and his wife living in the capital. [Character rough sketch]
"Normally, the sleeves of the bamboo cutter's formal wear wouldn't be this long, but I made it more in the feel of a person from the country who has admired city people and is trying to imitate them."

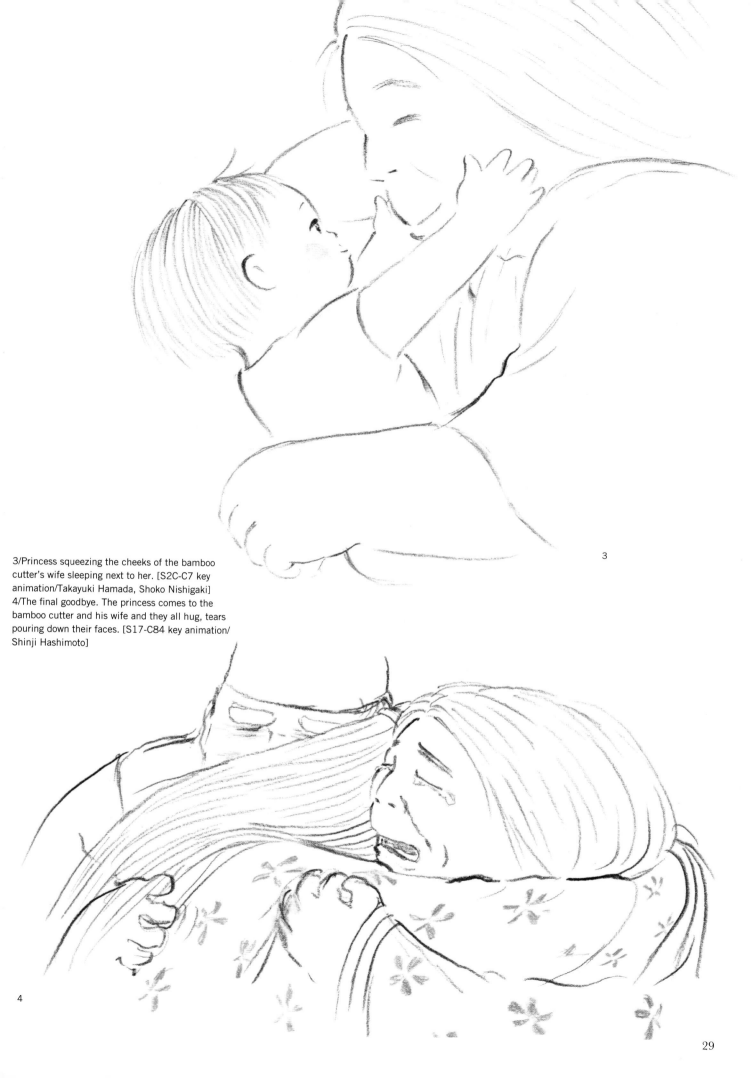

3/Princess squeezing the cheeks of the bamboo cutter's wife sleeping next to her. [S2C-C7 key animation/Takayuki Hamada, Shoko Nishigaki]

4/The final goodbye. The princess comes to the bamboo cutter and his wife and they all hug, tears pouring down their faces. [S17-C84 key animation/ Shinji Hashimoto]

3

4

基本は
こんなマユモ

Sutemaru

The princess's childhood friend and a big brother to the children of the mountain.

1/Sutemaru in his boyhood (age 13). [Character rough sketch]
"At first, I drew him with closely cropped hair to mark him as a child of the mountains (see page 14), but it seemed unlikely that they had clippers at the time that could shave his head so neatly [*laughs*], so I gave up on that. He grew up in the mountains, and I wanted to express that vitality. I gave him something like naturally curly hair, thick and coarse. I made his eyebrows thick and his lashes black."
2/Sutemaru's first appearance. He happens to be passing by and sees the parent wild boar racing toward the princess, so he drops his basket and starts running. [S2D-C13 layout revision]

3/After saving the princess in the nick of time, Sutemaru lifts his face and watches the danger recede. [S2D-C18 layout revision]
4/Princess tries to take a melon from a melon patch but has trouble with the vine. Sutemaru quickly cuts it away with a small knife. [S3C-C5 layout revision]
5/Sutemaru falls off a cliff chasing a pheasant. The pheasant is caught under him. He grabs it by the neck and slowly lifts it up. [S4-C20 key animation/Takayuki Hamada, Masako Sato]

3

4

5

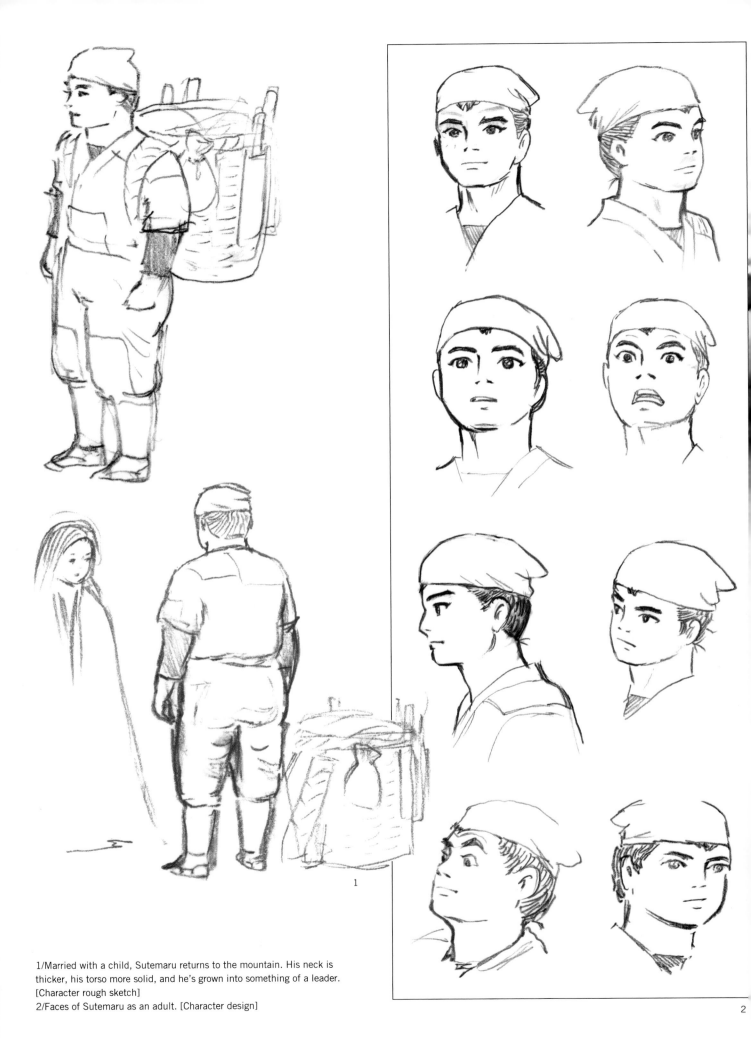

1/Married with a child, Sutemaru returns to the mountain. His neck is thicker, his torso more solid, and he's grown into something of a leader. [Character rough sketch]
2/Faces of Sutemaru as an adult. [Character design]

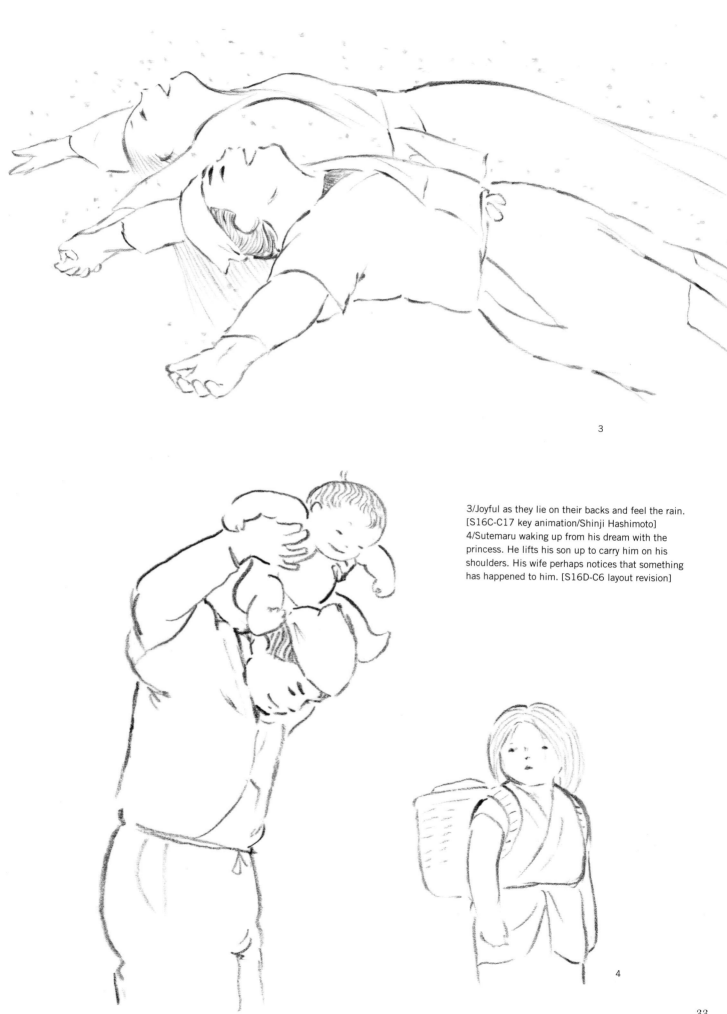

3

3/Joyful as they lie on their backs and feel the rain. [S16C-C17 key animation/Shinji Hashimoto]
4/Sutemaru waking up from his dream with the princess. He lifts his son up to carry him on his shoulders. His wife perhaps notices that something has happened to him. [S16D-C6 layout revision]

4

Children of the mountain

Children from the settlement of lathe turners near the bamboo cutter's house.
The boys are named Kou, Otsu, and Hei; the girls are Kare, Ro, and Jin.

1/Children of the mountain. The girls on the bottom right, from left to
right, are Ro, Kare, and Jin. [Character rough sketch]
"Ro is a character I drew when we were working on *Komoriuta no Tanjo*.
For Kare's hairstyle, I referenced a member of S#arp, a Korean pop group
I was listening to at the time."

1

2/Boys walking as they sing children's songs. From right to left, they are Kou
Hei, Hei's little brother, and Otsu. [S2D-C26 key animation/Takayuki Hamad
"Hamada drew this as a rough key animation, but I thought the linework was
interesting, so I used it as is in the animation."

2

3/The children mark out the rhythm with their whole bodies as they chant "Li'l Bamboo! Li'l Bamboo!" at the princess as she starts to walk. [S2B-C47 key animation/Takayuki Hamada]
4, 5/Princess starts walking toward the children and falls on her backside halfway there. The children react with exaggerated disappointment. [S2B-C44 layout revision]
"Of the three boys, Kou's face has a little more ego to it, but it ended up being more feigning innocence."

Me no Warawa

A lady attendant who takes care of the princess during her life in the capital. A girl of the same age as the princess.

1/Me no Warawa. [Character design]
"At first, she was simply the princess's attendant and had something more like a normal girl's face, but while I was redrawing her, her bangs, eyes, and mouth all ended up as horizontal lines. Takahata thought this was funny and gave her more scenes than she had originally. The rest of the crew would tell me that she was cuter than the princess. [laughs]"

2/She staggers along with a package on her head stuffed with letters like flags. [S10-C10 layout revision]

3, 4/She secretly appears, yanks up the traditional long skirt, and puts it on her own waist. [S7-C1 key animation/Shinpei Kamada]

5/Carrying a wooden brush and dish, Me no Warawa turns back to the princess and offers her the brush. [S9-C8 key animation/ layout revision]

6/Me no Warawa quietly fixing the hems of the nobles. [S10-C64 layout revision]

7/She comes running in to report that the crowd in front of the house is gone. [S10-C85 key animation/Yoshihiro Osugi]

8/Me no Warawa carries a tray and neatly slips through curtains around the platform where the princess is sitting. [S7-C53 key animation/Takayuki Hamada]

9/Me no Warawa belting out a children's song with the children. [S17-C60 key animation/Hideki Hamasu]

Lady Sagami

A leading lady the bamboo cutter calls from the palace to educate the mountain princess in the ways of a noble princess.

1/Lady Sagami. [Character design]
"I drew Lady Sagami as the stereotypical Heian beauty. I made sure to give her features so that she wouldn't be mistaken for the princess from a distance."
2/"A noble princess does not open her mouth and laugh." Lady Sagami chides the princess without showing her emotions. [S7-C9 key animation/Ayako Hata]
3/Princess running in front of Lady Sagami, disobeying her. Lady Sagami reels, stunned. [S7-C15 key animation/Ayako Hata]
4/Lady Sagami explaining a scroll to the princess. [S6-C4 layout revision]

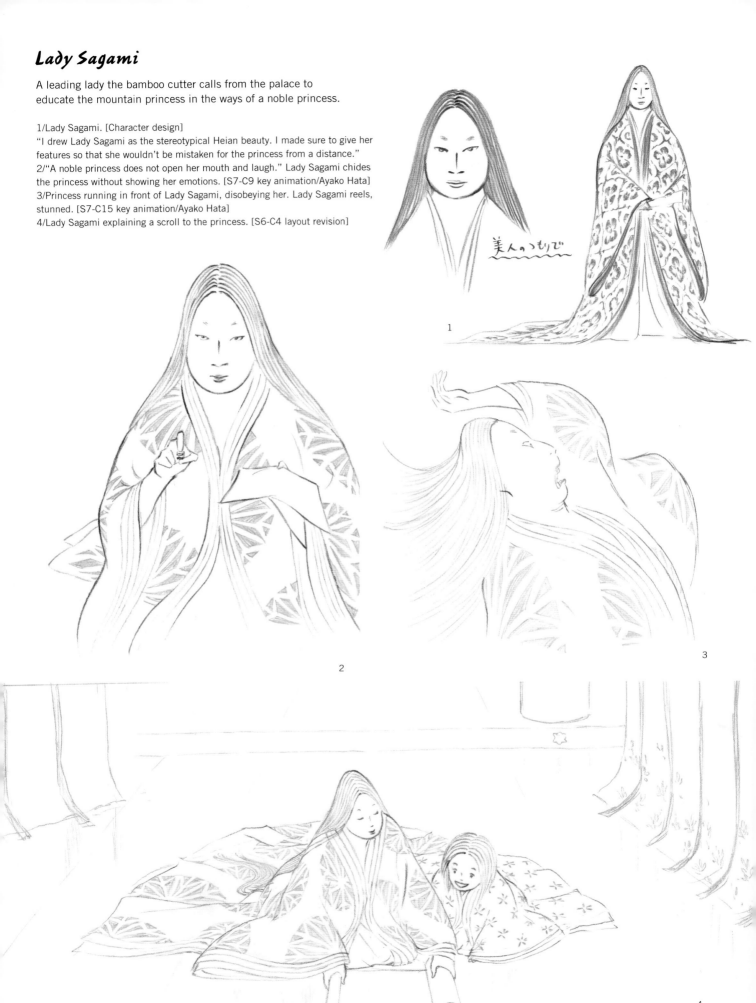

美人のつもりで

1

2

3

4

Inbe no Akita

An elderly man the bamboo cutter asks to be the princess's "name father." Cultivated with a good aesthetic sense.

6

7

5

8

5/Inbe no Akita in formal wear. [Character design]
"I didn't have a particular model for him. I drew him in the image of a cultivated older man."
6, 7/Inbe no Akita shaking with emotion the first time he meets Princess Kaguya. [S10-C26 layout revision]
8/Inbe no Akita listening to the princess playing the koto. [S7-36 layout revision]

Elderly charcoal maker

An old man the princess meets in the remains of the lathe turners' settlement. He is making charcoal.

11

9

10

9/Old man talking about the mountain after the princess asks where the lathe turners went. [S8-C26 key animation/Takayuki Hamada, Atsushi Tamura]
10/Old man turns toward the princess, but she's already gone. [S8-C33 key animation/Takayuki Hamada, Atsushi Tamura]
11/Old man doesn't stop working. [S8-C23 layout revision]
"With the bandana, he seems like a modern potter. I realized afterward that he looks like Shige from *My Neighbors the Yamadas*. [*laughs*]"

Prince Kuramochi

One of Princess Kaguya's suitors. He describes his joy at a marriage to the princess as "if I plucked a branch of the tree of jewels that grows on the Mountain of Horai, whose trunk is of gold and whose fruits are the whitest of pearls."

1/Prince Kuramochi in formal dress. [Character design]
"Prince Kuramochi is the picture of the general Heian noble."
2/Carrying a bamboo rack on his back, Prince Kuramochi comes along carrying a large treasure draped in silk. [S13A-C31 key animation/Emi Kamiishi]
3/Prince Kuramochi depicting exactly how he got the jeweled branch of Horai. [S13A-C59 key animation/Yoshihiro Osugi]
4, 5/Prince Kuramochi impersonating the angel he met on the beautiful mountain and his joy at discovering that the mountain is Mount Horai. [S13A-C63 key animation/Yoshihiro Osugi]

Minister of the Right Abe

One of Princess Kaguya's suitors. He describes the princess as "a robe of fire-rat fur, from which, when thrown into the fire, all impurity is burned away but which itself is not consumed, only shining more brightly as the flames grow higher." Also referred to as Lord Abe.

6/Minister of the Right Abe in formal dress. [Character rough sketch]
7/A proud Lord Abe shows off the robe of fire-rat fur. [S13B-C7 key animation/Toshio Kawaguchi]
8/The robes do not burn when put to flames…or they shouldn't. [S13B-C36 key animation/Toshio Kawaguchi, Shinpei Kamada]
9/He drops to his knees when they burn in the blink of an eye. [S13B-C41 key animation/Toshio Kawaguchi, Kumiko Kawana, Yuka Matsumura]

7

6

8

9

Middle Counselor Isonokami

One of Princess Kaguya's suitors. The most humble and gentle of the five. He describes the princess as "like the warm cowry shell amulet swallows use as a charm for a safe birth. That is a true treasure." Also referred to as Lord Isonokami.

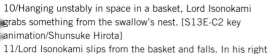

10

10/Hanging unstably in space in a basket, Lord Isonokami grabs something from the swallow's nest. [S13E-C2 key animation/Shunsuke Hirota]
11/Lord Isonokami slips from the basket and falls. In his right hand, a chick chirps energetically. [S13E-C5 layout revision]
12/Middle Counselor Isonokami in formal dress. [Character design]

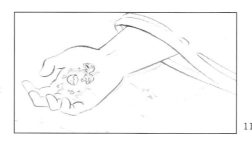

11

12

Grand Counselor Otomo

One of Princess Kaguya's suitors. He is short-tempered and likes fighting. He describes the princess as "a jewel that shines intensely from above, a gem with more radiance that the five-colored jewel that shines on the dragon's neck." Also referred to as Lord Otomo.

1/Grand Counselor Otomo in formal dress.
[Character rough sketch]
"I first drew him in the image of musician and actor Ryudo Uzaki. Takahata told me to make him look stronger, the kind of person who might kill someone, so he ended up like this."
2/The sea that attacks the ship with Lord Otomo aboard. The rain clouds that puff up take on the shape of a dragon. [S13C-C11 key animation /Tatsuzo Nishita]
3/A boatman on the ship. [S13C-C4 layout revision]
"This boatman was originally one of the designs for Grand Counselor Otomo, but I didn't use it in the end. When I thought about using it for someone else, it became the boatman."

1

2

4/Drenched in the waves, his topknot comes undone, leaving his hair loose and disheveled.
[S13C-C21 key animation/Hiroyuki Morita, Atsushi Tamura]

3

4

Prince Ishitsukuri

One of Princess Kaguya's suitors. He tells the princess, "I will worship you morning and night, with my forehead pressed to the ground in utter devotion. You are a treasure I would revere as much as the stone begging bowl of Lord Buddha himself."

5/Prince Ishitsukuri in formal dress. [Character rough sketch]
"When he first comes seeking the princess's hand, he has a bit of facial hair, but when he comes to her alone, I got rid of that hair and gave him a fresher look."
6/The prince invites the princess by saying, "Come with me to somewhere that is not here!" He freezes with the lively look on his face. [S13D-C23 revision by supervising animator/Kenichi Konishi]
7/The prince looking back from below as he begins to speak eloquently to the princess. [S13D-C12 key animation/Kazutaka Ozaki]
8/The prince's lawful wife appears in front of him with a hideous face. [S13D-C24 key animation/ Kazutaka Ozaki]
9/The prince being interrogated by his wife. [Character rough sketch]

5

6

7

9

8

The emperor

When he learns of Princess Kaguya, he is sure she wishes to be with him, so he tries to make her a lady of the court, but...

1/The emperor in formal dress. [Character design]
"I wanted him to have the most handsome face. For a while, I thought about making the character I drew as Prince Ishitsukuri the emperor. When I was wrestling with this, though, Takahata said to me, 'What if you made him a handsome man but with the balance off in one place? Like his chin or something.' This is what I settled on. Shichinosuke Nakamura, the voice actor who plays him, also has a young voice, so he ended up seeming even more noble and pure. His outfit is my own design, a rearrangement of the traditional ceremonial outfit sokutai."
2/The emperor embracing Princess Kaguya from behind while she is absorbed in playing the koto. [S14-C40 key animation/Miwa Sasaki]

1

2

Lathe turners

The lathe turners are artisans who make their living producing wooden objects like bowls. Sutemaru and the mountain children were born in their settlement.

1/Sutemaru's mother using a chisel to carve out the inside as she turns the bowl with her feet. [S3A-C14 layout revision]
2/Using a hatchet to finish the rough block cut from the wood to make a bowl. [S3A-C11 layout revision]
3/Sutemaru's older brother using a hand pulley. Sutemaru's father shaving wood with a plane. [S3A-C13 layout revision]
4/Carrying the finished bowls on his back to sell in the city. [S3A-C18 key animation/Ayako Hata]

2

4

1

3

People of the capital

One corner of the main road, in front of the temple gates. A carriage passes through the midst of the many people coming and going and the pigeons flying around. [S10-C103 layout revision]

People of the moon

The full moon shines brightly in the eastern sky the night of August 15, and many people from the moon fly down on clouds colored in pale light.

1/The moon king standing quietly.
[S17-C19 key animation/Tatsuzo Nishita]
2/The clouds with the party from the moon approach the ground and make everything clear.
[S17-C16 key animation/Tatsuzo Nishita]
"The people of the moon are mainly characters Takahata and Yoshiyuki Momose created together. I couldn't draw the moon king's face very well, and I struggled with it for a long time. The face that Momose drew really had that supernatural feel, so I basically used it as is."

1

2

3

4

Apsaras

Celestial beings that dance through the sky. They dance around the princess collapsed in the snow, and when the people of the moon come, they display mysterious powers.

3/Celestial maidens play their instruments while arrows turn into flowers and fall. [S17-C17 key animation/Tatsuzo Nishita]
4/Bright, cheerful music being played on a variety of instruments. [S17-C18 key animation/Tatsuzo Nishita]

5

6

5, 6/Apsaras dancing beautifully and cheerfully. [Character rough sketch] "[Atsushi] Tamura drew a lot of the apsara shots for me."

Birth	1–4 [S1-C22] The girl smiles at the bamboo cutter, but quickly yawns and falls asleep.
	5 [S1-C24] The girl enveloped in a white light, sleeping.
	6 [S1-C25] "What a beautiful princess!"
	7–9 [S1-C27] He scoops her up with his hands very carefully, being careful not to shake her.
	10 [S1-C43] The bamboo cutter's wife looks at the girl sleeping in the bamboo cutter's hands.
	11–14 [S1-C44] She awakes from her sleep and suddenly starts moving, reaching out in a big stretch. [Key animation/Miwa Sasaki]

Scene Gallery

A number of scenes were selected from the film *The Tale of the Princess Kaguya*, and directing animator Osamu Tanabe selected a few especially appealing frames from these. Animators pay attention to each and every frame, which flash by in an instant in the movie. Introduced here are the time, effort, and trouble as well as the beauty of the images themselves.

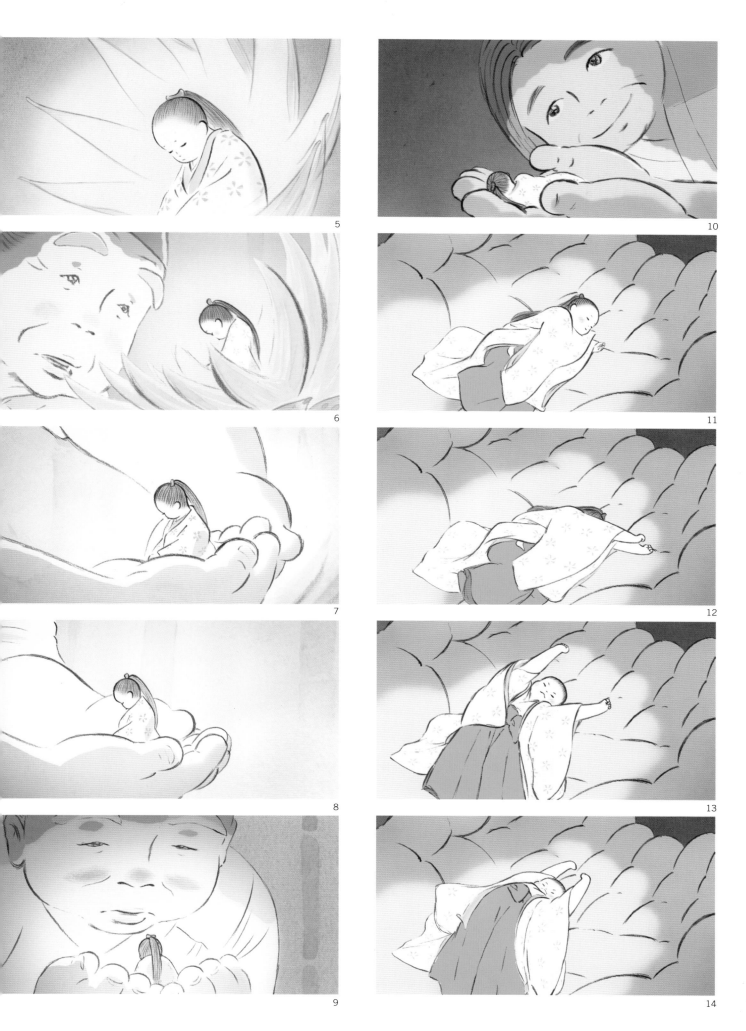

5

6

7

8

9

10

11

12

13

14

Rolling around

1–19 [S2B-C11] The baby rolls around and around. In the end, she rolls onto her back and looks straight ahead. What is she looking at?
[Key animations/Takayuki Hamada]

5

1

6

2

3

8

4

9

10

11

12

13

14

15

16

17

18

19

The princess and the wild boar piglets

1, 2 [S2D-C7] Noticing the princess, the piglets trot backward in a row.
3 [S2D-C8] They stare at the princess in a perfect row.
4 [S2D-C9] The princess cries out, "Come here!"
5, 6 [S2D-C10] When she gently reaches out a hand, the piglets come to her one after the other, perhaps because of her mysterious power.
7–9 [S2D-C11] The princess pets the piglets as they lick her. Notice that one of the piglets has fallen over.
[Key animations/Shoko Nishigaki]

5

1

6

2

7

3

8

4

9

Uncontrollable rage and violent emotion

1–3 [S7-C71], 4 [S7-C74], 5, 6 [S7-C75], 7 [S7-C77] Knocking down the door, racing through the gate, and flying from the manor because of her intense anger and grief.
8–11 [S7-C78A], 12–17 [S7-C78B] She sheds layers of ceremonial kimono and charges down the main road of the capital.
18 [S7-C79], 19 [S7-C80] Her face, a mix of anger and sadness.
20–23 [S7-C82], 24, 25[S7-C83], 26–28 [S7-C84], 29 [S7-C85] She races through a field, charges up a mountain road, and keeps running.
[Key animations/Shinji Hashimoto]

5

1

6

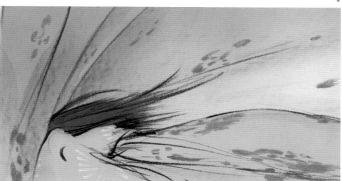

2

7

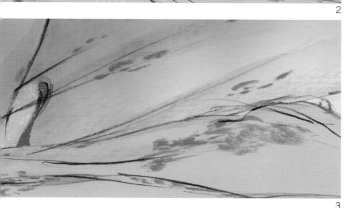

3

8

4

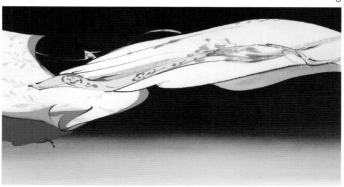

9

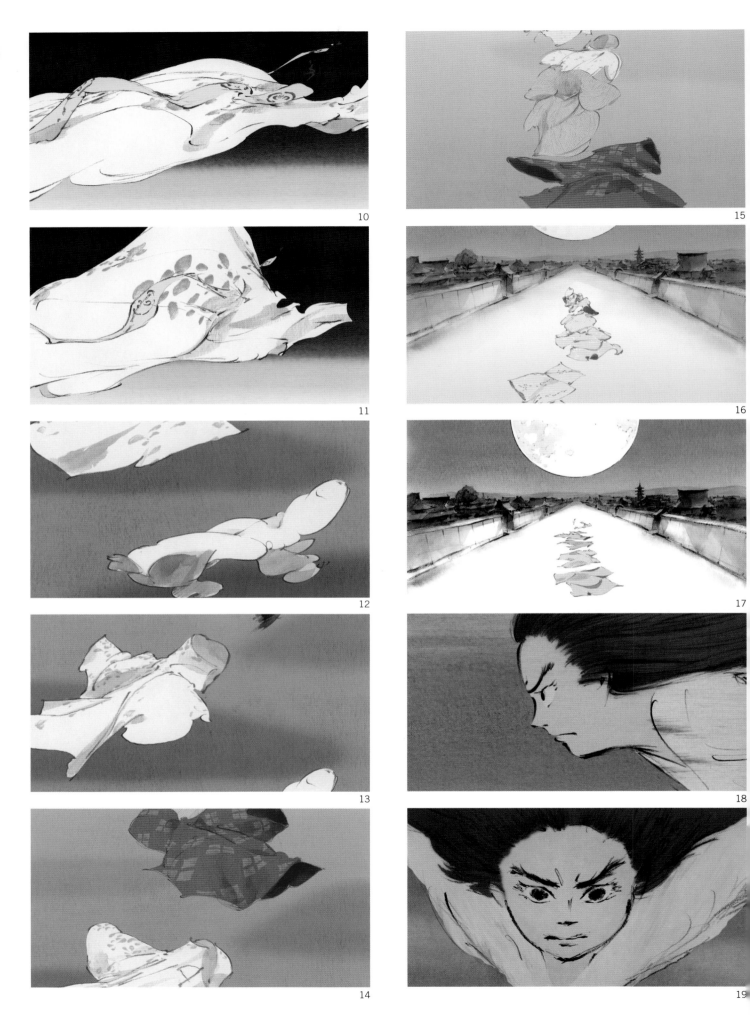

20

21

22

23

24

25

26

27

28

29

Me no Warawa's misfortune

1 [S10-C1], 2 [S10-C2], 3 [S10-C3] Seeing the crowd in front of the house, Me no Warawa is troubled.

4, 5 [S10-C5], 6 [S10-C6] The men notice Me no Warawa and run over to her.

7–9 [S10-C7] The men step on a fallen man to get to Me no Warawa.

10–14 [S10-C9] She ends up crushed by the letters addressed to Princess Kaguya being thrust at her.

15–19 [S10-C10] She goes to the princess, carrying her large bundle. She hands over the sakura branch she brought.

[Key animations/Takayuki Hamada]

5

1

6

2

7

3

8

4

9

10

11

12

13

14

15

16

17

18

19

Going to the mountain sakura

1–4 [S11-C11] The princess excitedly runs up the mountain path. As she runs, she lifts up her kimono and starts to stumble, but catches herself.
5–9 [S11-C12] Running straight toward the sakura tree. Flower petals dance in the air around her.
[Key animations/Shinji Hashimoto]

5

1

6

2

7

3

8

4

9

Tying up her hair

1 [S13A-C12] She sets a grasshopper free in the garden after it wanders into the outbuilding.
2–9 [S13A-C15] She pulls up her now-long hair, twists it up on her head, and pins it down.
[Key animations/Masashi Ando]

1

2

3

4

5

6

7

8

9

Fake

1 [S13E-C10], 2 [S13E-C12] Princess Kaguya stands in the garden at dusk.
3–6 [S13E-C13], 7 [S13E-C14], 8–13 [S13E-C15], 14 [S13E-C17] She picks up a scythe and clears away the grass.
15 [S13E-C19], 16 [S13E-C20], 17 [S13E-C21], 18, 19 [S13E-C22] She kicks away the small house, bridge, and water wheel set on the hill, crying "Fake!"
20, 21 [S13E-C23], 22 [S13E-C25] The bamboo cutter's wife stops her. The princess moans that it's her fault everyone is miserable.
23–25 [S13E-C26], 26, 27 [S13E-C27] The bamboo cutter's wife listens to the princess and her feelings.
28 [S13E-C28], 29 [S13E-C29] The two hug. The full moon shines in the sky.
[Key animations/Shinji Hashimoto]

5

1

6

2

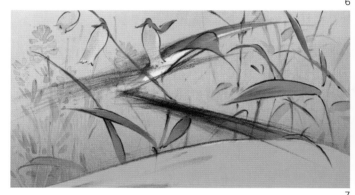

7

3

8

4

9

10

11

12

13

14

15

16

17

18

19

61

20

21

22

23

24

25

26

27

28

29

Art

The art in *The Tale of the Princess Kaguya* was drawn by the art staff, led by Kazuo Oga, based on the intentions of director Isao Takahata, making use of Osamu Tanabe's characters and the specifications of the animation design. This section is divided into three parts—interviews, production imageboards, and background art—which depict the birth of animation art in watercolors that deliberately leaves out detail, a clear departure from the detailed backgrounds in poster paints of conventional Studio Ghibli works.

Art Director
Kazuo Oga

Backgrounds with a breeziness, not too faint or light, drawn leaving natural blank spaces

Kazuo Oga: Born February 1952 in Akita prefecture. He started working at the animation background art company Kobayashi Production in 1972. He first did the backgrounds on *Pinocchio: The Series* (1972), and subsequently did the backgrounds for a number of animated works under Shichiro Kobayashi. In 1975, he left Kobayashi Production, and then returned in 1977 to work on the theatrical releases *Unico* (1981) and *Cobra* (1982) before leaving the company again in 1982. At the invitation of Takamura Mukuo, art director for the feature-length *Harmagedon: Genma taisen* (1983), he joined the project. He then worked as the art director for theatrical releases produced by Madhouse, including *Barefoot Gen* (1983), *Toki no Tabibito: Time Stranger* (1986), and *Wicked City* (1987). In 1987, through an introduction from Nizo Yamamoto, art director for *Grave of the Fireflies* (1988), he joined the production of *My Neighbor Totoro* (1988), directed by Hayao Miyazaki. He was the art director for the Studio Ghibli films *Only Yesterday* (1991) and *Pom Poko* (1994), and a co-art director on *Princess Mononoke* (1997). After working on *Whisper of the Heart* (1995), he became a freelance artist and has worked on the background art for a great number of animated works, but *The Tale of the Princess Kaguya* is his first time as art director in the sixteen years since *Princess Mononoke*. He has also worked on picture books and illustrations, and in 2006, he directed the DVD film *Taneyamagahara no Yoru*. The exhibit Ghibli Eshokunin Kazuo Oga (*Ghibli Craftsman Kazuo Oga*), which has toured Japan since summer 2007, has welcomed over one million visitors.

Kazuo Oga, art director for *The Tale of the Princess Kaguya*, has worked as the art director on films for both Hayao Miyazaki and Isao Takahata. In recent years, he has been involved in the production of films not as an art director but as one of the background artists, and has been active in a wide range of areas including picture books and illustrations. It has been sixteen years since he worked as one of the art directors for *Princess Mononoke*. In this interview, we discuss how the frontlines of animation have changed in that time with the overall digitization of the industry.

First of all, can you tell us about the sequence of events that led to you agreeing to be the art director for *The Tale of the Princess Kaguya*?

Oga: Since the time my exhibition of Studio Ghibli Backgrounds (*Ghibli Eshokunin Kazuo Oga, 2007–2010*) was touring the country, I'd been hearing rumors that Takahata was working on a new project. I'm pretty sure I first heard about it directly at the Niigata exhibit in 2009, although they weren't sounding me out at that point.

At the last stop on the tour, the Kobe exhibit, the producer Nishimura asked me to come take a look at Takahata's work. When I went, there were still only two or so desks in what they called the preparation room, and Takahata and animator Tanabe [Osamu] were in the middle of a meeting. Takahata showed me a gorgeous book of art with enlarged images from *Ban Dainagon Emaki*, and told me, "It's so interesting to enlarge something small. You can really see the roughness of the lines drawn by the brush and the traces of the mistakes." He was emphasizing how fascinating it could be to enlarge a picture that had been drawn small.

After that, we all went to a café and Takahata talked for another couple of hours about *The Tale of the Bamboo Cutter* and all kinds of things about the Heian era, but neither the director nor the producer said what kind of role they wanted me to play. So I was thinking that I could maybe help out as one of the background artists and wondering how I could say no if they wanted me for art director. But I couldn't since the meeting ended without any formal offer. [*laughs*] I actually was one of five art directors for *Princess Mononoke*, and I was already working at home then. The last time I worked in the studio was on *Whisper of the Heart*, and it had been nearly

twenty years since then, so I figured it would be hard for me at that point to wrangle a large art staff in the studio.

In the end, you did accept the job.

Oga: After I visited the prep room, Nishimura said he would drive me home. I don't particularly like being driven home, so I told him I'd take the train. But he pushed and eventually wore me down. On the way, he told me that Takahata's health wasn't great and that this would probably be his last film. We talked about how I could maybe do it if I could work alone in my studio. He had supper at my house before heading home himself. For a while after that, I was helping out with *The Secret World of Arrietty*, but Nishimura watched for when that was finished and brought Takahata to my house. When the director himself comes to your house to ask you, you really can't say no anymore, can you? [*laughs*]

Of course, Takahata had been very good to me up to that point, so I wanted to help in the spirit of paying back that debt. I was only supposed to be working on the mountain chapter at first. Nishimura said that if it was just the part in the first half about the mountains where the princess spends her childhood, then I could probably draw it by myself at home. Meaning that I would only spend that much time on production. I thought that this film would take three or four years to create, five at most, and that it would be nice to be able to take my time and draw without commuting to the studio. That didn't happen in the end, of course. [*laughs*]

In June 2010, the studio for *The Tale of the Princess Kaguya* (Studio Kaguya) was opened, and production went into full force. But when did you actually start work?

Oga: I was on *Arrietty* until around April, and then I had some picture-book work, so it was from about October, I guess. Until the new Studio No. 7 started operation in February two years later, I was drawing at home the whole time. I just couldn't make a decision about going into the studio where so many members of the staff were. About once a week, I'd take in the things I'd drawn and have the director take a look.

That went on for a while.

Later, we ended up making the pilot film, and I got a request from the director to draw a large background where the bamboo cutter was walking among trees drawn by Tanabe.

1

2

1/Scenery around the bamboo cutter's house taken from an artboard done in the initial stages of production. This was done with a level of detail closer to previous art, and from there, the crew investigated how to remove that detail.
2/Mountain bushes and grasses.

So I figured I would get ready before we started the actual work. I went to Kyoto for research. I got my son to drive and we rented a car. I looked at the plants and terrain around Ohara, the mountain streams and ravines, took a lot of photos.

It wasn't so much that I wanted to reference a particular place; rather, I felt like it might be useful in thinking about the atmosphere of the mountain chapter as a whole. Later, it turned out that I just had to make sure I didn't draw anything that wasn't there in that time period, so I drew the things I saw there not in the production imageboard but in something like the imageboard of the stage before that.

What's distinctive about the background art for this film is your style of drawing. You deliberately don't put in color, you leave those blank spaces. Was this Takahata's aim right from the beginning?

Oga: I joined the production after it started, and Takahata and Tanabe had already set that policy in the imageboard and storyboards. The idea was to not draw the details so as to make the overall art style breezy, to make use of the blank spaces where the lines slipped or weren't filled in, like in ink drawings done with brushes, for both the animated characters and the background art. The imageboard pieces Tanabe originally did were on fairly small pages. When they were enlarged for photography, the lines would be thicker, the roughness and force of the brush would come out, for the interesting flavor of the enlarged images of *Ban Dainagon Emaki* that Takahata showed me. This was the movie's fundamental concept from the start.

For me, this was still rough since it was the imageboard stage, but I thought it might be better to draw a little more detail in the background images. In the early days, I didn't go with how small the frame was. Instead, I drew in a dense style like normal at a regular size, but I was told that this film wasn't like that. Even with pictures I thought I'd done simply, Takahata would enlarge a spot with a lot of space and show me a copy before telling me that I could get rid of more color or detail.

So it isn't like they were suddenly backgrounds, complete works of art. I shifted my style of drawing and checked Takahata and Tanabe's reactions, which allowed me to slowly get closer to what they were looking for. Even with images I'd drawn with the intention of being more relaxed than usual, Takahata and Tanabe would make these faces, like it was all still totally standard. I tried all kinds of styles as we went through this. Tanabe's imageboard was a really important reference for me, and I was always aiming for background art that matched the mood of his drawings.

For the backgrounds in the capital in the second half, the way the buildings and things are so boldly abbreviated is really striking.

Oga: Takahata said that there are basically no references other than picture scrolls for the buildings and streets of the Heian era, and nobody's seen them, so he wanted to draw them quite quite roughly, without much emphasis. He wanted to draw the mountain scenes in great detail, make them very appealing and connected with the theme of the film: that the princess doesn't want to go back to the moon because life in the mountains with Sutemaru and everyone else is so much fun. This was Takahata's thinking, and since I couldn't make them too rough, the images in the mountain chapter have more color and detail than the capital chapter.

As an actual problem here, at the stage when production was moving forward, I'd been researching historical items, and drawing the city from the Heian days was a lot of work and took a lot of time, so I stopped. Takahata and Tanabe had already been collecting and examining references for years for this film, and the storyboard had been done based on that. Plus, I had Tanabe's imageboard. So I started thinking I could just ask them if I didn't know something.

For both the mountain and the capital chapters, I got all kinds of inspiration from Tanabe's unique images. I was careful to draw lines with roughness and different weights, but if I let my guard down for even a second, I ended up with a bunch of boring, uniform lines. With Tanabe's imageboard, he had this quite interesting way of drawing. For instance, he'd put thicker lines at the border with the floor at the base of the pillars in the mansion in the capital. Or he'd make the line on one side of the bamboo in the front of the bamboo forest thick to produce a sense of perspective. And it wasn't just the lines. There were places where his use of color was really fresh. I think this is Tanabe's own sensibility, and for me, there was a sense of everything being neatly tucked away. I regret that I couldn't really get close to him. Takayuki Hamada said it's best not to say your regrets out loud, though. [*laughs*]

So it was about not drawing too much and keeping it from being too dense, which meant that you yourself had to incorporate a drawing style different from what you had used up to that point.

Oga: It wasn't just me—this was hard for all of the background staff. When I had them draw more freely in this rough style, I think we got some carefree images with their own individual flavors. But with the requirement of backgrounds for animation, there were of course certain conventions we had to follow, and you could never really get that free, spontaneous line. With this film, Takahata was aiming to have the allure of lines drawn with brushes like in picture scrolls or ink paintings. This isn't something you can just sit down and churn out.

The ideal was a line that was drawn easily in one stroke, with a natural power, that would make its appeal felt even more when enlarged. But the lines carefully drawn bit by bit to make it look like that don't turn into lines with much allure when enlarged. And since the background layouts drawn by the animators had explanatory text and unnecessary lines, I had the art staff responsible for each scene redraw the original art for the background and examine this way of using the line. We'd copy this onto animation paper for the rough copy. The original lines basically didn't change moving onto the photograph copy, and even if something seemed like a bit of a mistake, it could be easily fixed with some color, so we didn't draw the art from square one.

That's a serious strength of this film, making use of the line like this.

Oga: With the poster colors we usually used, the lines would be ruined or hidden, so we used transparent watercolors.

However, even if they had used transparent watercolors in dashed-off sketches, this was the first time any of the staff was drawing all the backgrounds for a feature-length film with them, and they all had a hard time with it. The best thing is to be able to do it roughly in one stroke. Even if there's some irregularity on the page, it could become part of the charm. But these paints might be faint in color, and the color will get heavy and dirty if you paint over something a number of times. It was all fine and good to paint in one go and get some nice blank spaces, but later, we'd realize that there wasn't

3

4

3, 4/Initial art boards of the forest where the princess spends time with Sutemaru and the children. Both have the same composition, but the drawing style was changed to be in line with the perspective Takahata was aiming for.

enough blank space, or the overall look was good but we wanted about this much more blank space in this part here. At times like that, I had them draw it over right from the start, with the idea that they should use as many animation pages as it took without worrying about the waste.

These intentional blank spaces are one of the distinguishing features of this background art. Were there any specifications on how to draw them?

Oga: We left that to the sensibility of the people drawing. Takahata wasn't giving images the okay because the blank spaces were like this or like that—the decision was being made based on the overall lightness of the image, which was impacted by those blank spaces. So there were no rules about shape or size, but blank spaces that were the same size or symmetrical weren't interesting. Like I said earlier, with an image drawn loosely like a rough sketch, those spaces won't be the same size or have a symmetrical shape to start with. One other difficult thing was with normal backgrounds, the ends of the brushstrokes and painting are all outside of the frame, but this time we had to leave them in the frame, and on top of that, make them look like part of the picture. This was an entirely different way of doing things, so everyone on staff had to work really hard here.

Since I needed them to draw in this style of a single brushstroke to leave those blank spaces and to use paints (transparent watercolors) that they weren't too familiar with, for about a month after joining the crew, I'd have new background artists practice copying the imageboard to get familiar with the way of using the brush and the way of adding color. Even still, if they were overly conscious of it, no matter how nice it ended up looking, you could feel something deliberate in it. Human techniques in the end just can't beat something that springs up organically like the blank spaces from a brush made in the force of the moment.

You can't know what kind of effect a blank space is going to have until you draw it. You can paint it all white later with poster colors and draw in the blank spaces, but it's totally different. We tried all kinds of things. It was a little better when we painted with watercolor crayons and water, but I hated the way I could tell what part had been painted. In the end, I worked out a method of doing it: I would decide on how much blank space I wanted, add an opening to a place drawn in a faint line with a knife, cut away just that one part, and quickly peel it away. This was the white of the animation paper, so I could get a bit more of a natural-feeling blank space. I didn't just fix my own work like this; I did it to backgrounds drawn by the other artists, too. Whenever I pulled out a knife in front of them, though, they were shocked and wondered what exactly I was going to do. [*laughs*] I ended up using this method in all kinds of places.

A month of practice is not the norm, and the trick of making the blank spaces you mentioned is fascinating. But what was it that gave you personally the most trouble?

Oga: Like I said, although it was somewhat easier in the sense that there was a lot of blank space in the small frames so the area I had to cover with my drawing was smaller, there were some difficulties in getting the art in line with the director's policy of "draw quickly, lightly, and with a rough edge so it doesn't get boring." I felt like it wouldn't be an animation image if it was too faint or too light, so I added a little meat to Tanabe's images, and I incorporated a certain amount of density and depth, thinking that could be perfect.

In that sense, for this film, I wanted to forge an even deeper unity between the background and the characters, and I tried to get as close as possible to Tanabe's art style, but I'm not sure how far I managed to get with that. I might not have been able to do a good job on creating these rough, free lines; it might have just ended up being my own style of drawing.

Also, I hadn't worked in a studio for a long time, so with the proliferation of digital work in productions, I felt a bit like Urashima Taro returning from the bottom of the ocean. When we did the checks, the director and everyone else would peer into this tiny monitor, and I was surprised that we were making films in this kind of tight squeeze now. They say that colors are different from monitor to monitor, and with digital, you decide on color by numbers. I knew from experience that if you're using actual paints, then if you mix *this* color with *that* color, you'll get *this* kind of color, but I never got the chance to communicate that. I was a little worried that we would no longer be able to have a shared image of a color or imagine the subtle differences in colors.

Of course, there are advantages with digital, and it really did some heavy lifting. When we wanted to complete a single image, but it didn't look like we would make it in time in terms of the schedule, we could draw one part separately and fuse them together digitally. We can do that kind of thing now. We can't rely too heavily on digital, though, and it really does depend on how you use it, but now that I know this, I've gotten to reconsider all kinds of things, and I think it was an interesting job.

5

5–10/Initial art board drawn at the script stage before the screen composition was determined in storyboards and layouts. Some parts of the construction and style of drawing in the film were also decided here.

6

7

8

9

10

Kazuo Oga Art
Art Boards Gallery

As the art director who designed the art and led the staff drawing the backgrounds in the production of *The Tale of the Princess Kaguya*, Kazuo Oga drew a great number of pieces of art board. He set out the composition of the scenes, a unity between backgrounds and characters, and the coloring for the characters, among other things, as a reference for the crew to examine for the world of the film they were going to create. Some of the characters drawn in the art board were copied by Oga himself from the storyboards and layout, while some were colored with watercolors after cutting and pasting from key animations done by the animation staff. Much of the actual background art was redrawn based on these concept images, but some pieces were also used as is.

1

2

73

3

4

5

1, 2 (Comments are all by Kazuo Oga.) "Everyone knows the bamboo forest from the story of The Tale of the Bamboo Cutter, but since it appears in the first scene, I was thinking right from the initial stages about the look, what kind of style to use to create the right mood for the film, and I drew several pieces of concept art. Takahata said that 1 was best for how it gave a sense of distance with the thick fog in parts, and I moved forward with drawing the backgrounds for the film based on this image for the coloring. I started with little color in the scene wrapped in morning fog, so the green is a little strong, but in the actual film, I had them pull back on that a bit for a more relaxed coloring in photography."

3–5/"The girl is born in timber bamboo. Unlike moso and other bamboos, timber-bamboo shoots have distinctive flecks of color. I tried likening these to the pattern on an elaborate kimono. We all have this image of Princess Kaguya coming out of a bamboo stalk cut by the bamboo cutter, but in the original story, it doesn't say anything about cutting bamboo—the bamboo shines, and in the blink of an eye, she's born. So I think this way of drawing it in the film works really well."

6

6–11/"I based the bamboo cutter's house in 6 on a farmhouse I saw when I was doing research in Ohara in Kyoto. I don't actually know if this kind of house existed in this period. I created the dirt-floor interior (9, 10) by rearranging a rough layout drawn by Tanabe. This area has more of a blue to it in the film, but I think it would have been better if it were a little darker. There's the scene where the bamboo cutter and his wife are coming inside from the bright outdoors, so the shadows of the wooden door would be harder to make out.

"We flipped the orientation of the background in 7 and used it in the film. (Note: In the film, the people are facing this way, while the background has the slope descending from left to right.) Another of the many bamboo forests I drew is 8. Takahata asked if I couldn't have more gaps so that you could almost hear the rustling of the leaves, so I put in more gaps later."

7

8

9

10

78

11

12

12/"I did this piece pretty early on. It has more of a redness to it in the film, but Takahata decided that the coloring for that evening hour is basically like this."

13/"For the downpour scene, on top of creating several different kinds of art boards with ones that had tons of grass growing up from below and this much ground and grass, I also drew materials for double exposures to express the transparency of the puddles in photography."

14/"This was the initial image, but after I drew this piece, Takahata talked about wanting to have more leaves covering the front for a scene where the two of them are in a closed-off, secret space, so in the end, the grasses had more of a dense growth to them."

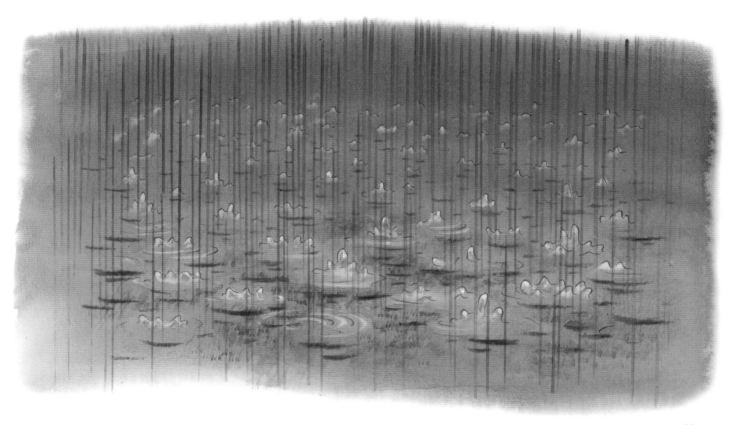

13

14

15/"This is inside the carriage, but the way the light hits is a little too sharp, and in the background in the film, it's a little hazier and darker. I did the background with paint to make it darker overall. The princess's kimono is a cel, so it seems heavy no matter how you look at it, but I think I was able to get a kind of halo by layering the paint to focus the light in front."

16, 17/"I drew these as variations on the coloring of the kimonos of the ladies who come to welcome the princess and the carriage. At first, the carriage was entirely black (17), but given that Princess Kaguya was riding in it, I made it green and added the bamboo leaf pattern (16). Tanabe thought of this design."

16

17

18

19

20

18–20/"The bamboo cutter's mansion is the setting for the story in the capital and an important element in deciding the style of the film, so Takahata put in a request to see how it would look if I drew Tanabe's imageboard as the background art. I drew the image (20) at home before I started in the studio. Takahata came to my house once, looked at this image and one other drawing, and indicated his interest in perhaps moving in this direction. In the actual background (P161), there's less color, and there's more gold popping out.

"As for the buildings of the capital, Takahata talked about how having that Heian-palace architecture in an image wouldn't be very interesting, so he was fine with making the passages a bit off or making the structure a bit strange. He said it was good so long as the scene itself was interesting and the art style was appealing. Which reminds me—we also talked about whether this mansion was new or if they bought it used and renovated it. When the princess first comes to the capital and she's running around delighted at how gorgeous the building is and how beautiful the kimono are, I colored it with a brightness like a new building. But it wasn't very interesting to make the pillars and everything shiny, so we ended up trying to give it a little more of an older air in later scenes."

23

21–23/"I drew 21 in the early stages. I tried having the princess's shadow projected onto the wall, but it seemed like having space here was better than having her shadow, so I ended up with her shadow a little hazy in the light of the flame in the final look of 22."

24–27/"I don't really know if the bamboo cutter's wife made the yard with the vegetable garden (24, 26) and the outbuilding (25) to be more settled in, or if she reworked what was already there, but this is a piece that I'd worked on right from the early stages, and the director told me that these would be important places in the latter half of the film. Since there is a lot of white with the scene outside left blank, I thought the kitchen would be good darker and more closed off, and I drew all four corners of it like this. For the vegetables planted in the field, I went with ones that could be judged to have been eaten by people of the time, taking the vegetables that can grow in winter noted in the *Manyōshū*. But when I wanted a different coloring, I slipped in something that looked like some kind of vegetable without a clearly defined shape. [*laughs*]"

26

27

89

28

28–30/"For 28, I read the script wrong and drew it with a daytime setting; then I redrew it later at dusk. In 30, the sky outside the house is still white, and it doesn't look like dusk, so I drew some cloud-like things to create that kind of atmosphere."

90

29

30

31

32

33

31–33/"I drew 31 when we made the pilot film. In the end, the color of the bamboo blind in front of her was changed from red to green. At first, Tanabe's imageboard had them drawn in red, but Takahata suggested we make it a more subdued color, so we changed it. There's something like a thin curtain hanging in front of her in 32. The source of light (the lamp) is behind the curtain. Normally, the curtain would be almost entirely white, but I decided to make just the center bright and drop the surrounding area into darkness.

"This isn't just here; there was a policy of making the light around the princess white rather than yellow. For the light of the bamboo in the birth scene, I had originally put some yellow in, but I later went with white because there was the influence of the world of the moon. I also made the moon itself uniformly white rather than yellow. Conversely, I gave earth things a warm coloring like from the light of a fire. At Tanabe's suggestion, I made the shadows gray rather than black. But since the screen would look a little sad if there was too much gray, I also put a certain amount of color into the shadows. The banquet scene was a difficult one, and it took a lot of work to handle the many characters. Even though I started work on it fairly early, I was working on it right up until the very end."

34

35

36

37

38

34–37/"The scene that 36 and 37 are for ended up being a famous one, and honestly, animator Shinji Hashimoto is really unopposed when it comes to this stuff. He originally expanded on this image from the storyboard and made it his own unique drawing, but it was simply too well done, so I used his key frame for the background. The work of the art department was to draw the sky and the moon. We had the thought that a little color somewhere in the background would be nice, so I added a little emerald green to the tree root and forest to get a balance with the princess's red hakama."

38–40/"Starting at the middle of the film, there are a lot more indoor scenes. These images came about from the thought that there was no need to draw the blinds and tables the same way every time. The room in 38 is a bit dim, and I did the coloring to match the sadness of the princess getting pushed along in a direction she doesn't want to go. Behind the blinds on the opposite side (the front), there is a gloom in the room that the light doesn't penetrate, so the rather thick black lines are a different way of drawing. Also, for the tables and things, we thought it might be fun to use the same patterns as the princess's kimono, and in 40, I embedded it with a pattern like sakura."

39

40

41

42

43

41–43/"I couldn't really decide on the coloring for the flower-viewing scene at the palace (41, 42). I had the kimono in green, but this overlapped with the greenery in the background, so in the end I changed them to blue tones. For the group scene in 43, I just went ahead and let the white fly. We drew the people in the back in art and had the finishing staff color them. When the background has no color, it's easier to decide on the character colors, but I was worried at first about the characters in white kimono on the white background. Once we got to this point, though, I was fine with it and stopped being bothered by it. [*laughs*]"

44, 45/"In the end, I changed the color of the kimono of the princess and Lady Sagami in 44 to green and purple respectively, but this is a piece of art board that Tanabe also liked. For 45, I had a wall behind the platform where the princess is, but Takahata said he wanted the space to have more depth, so I redrew it with pillars."

46, 47/"Since there's a series of buildings and interiors once she gets to the capital, I had a lot of fun drawing these two. I drew the flowers in front in 46 as the foreground (parts of the background placed in front of the background). Even with this, there needed to be white space, so I did the lines in white forms, and asked them to cut it out just like this. But then the white was too uniform and drew the eye, so I had them erase it later. I made the art staff and the photographer work so hard. It really is difficult to intentionally create white. But apparently there was still something missing for the director, and I ended up adding small white butterflies flying above the flowers."

44

45

46

47

48

49

50

51

48–51/"The garden in 51 was made so that the princess could remember her happy life in the mountains, and it's set up so that the grass looks like a forest if you lie down to look at it. For the central hill with the model house, I struggled with what kinds of things would grow there if left unattended for years. Takahata suggested that it might be fine if I didn't draw anything, but at the very last minute, it felt like something was missing, so I added a road."

52/"I had trouble deciding what to do about the colors of the individual jewels on the jeweled branch of Horai. I tried painting large gems any number of times, and I realized that if there was too little yellow, it felt sad overall. Each of the animators had their own way of drawing the branch and adding light, which was really interesting. In the end, we matched up the color for finishing and photography and had the coloring close to what was in the concept art."

53, 54/"For the stormy-sea scene, I struggled with how to differentiate the sea, the sky, and the clouds, so I got some help from animation and photography. We overlapped the three images I drew for backgrounds and added a little linework and movement in animation, allowing us to express the changes in the clouds. There's also a scene where the clouds get lit up by lightning, but I didn't create any lighting elements. When the white parts left unpainted in the picture were overlaid on the background, it gave birth to an unexpected result and made it look like the interior of the cloud was lit up."

55–58/"The scenes with a lot of shadow were difficult, but I think that the effect in 55 works quite well, with the bold shadows on the characters from the initial art board stage. It was supposed to be gloomy in 56, so I also dropped the pink of the princess's kimono and drew the scene with an overall low contrast. In the end, I made the grasses in front even darker and added some variation. For 57 and 58, I was initially thinking of blue and gray shadows, but Tanabe mentioned that he'd like to make the shadows red, so I went ahead and added a bright red to the falling shadows. I put in a little purple inside the room and made it so that it didn't ruin the overall atmosphere."

53

54

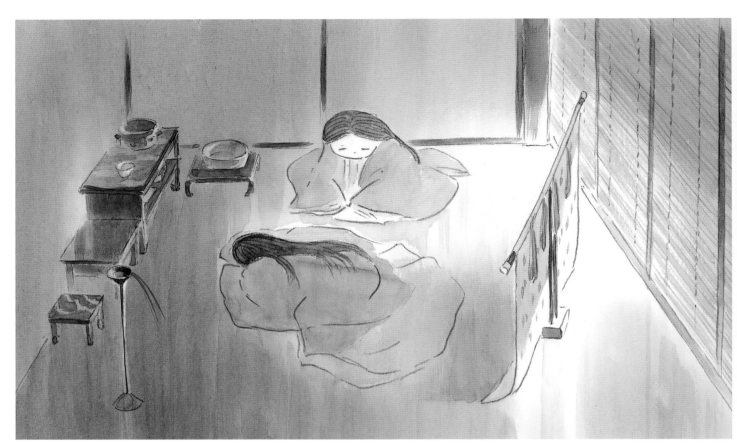

55

56

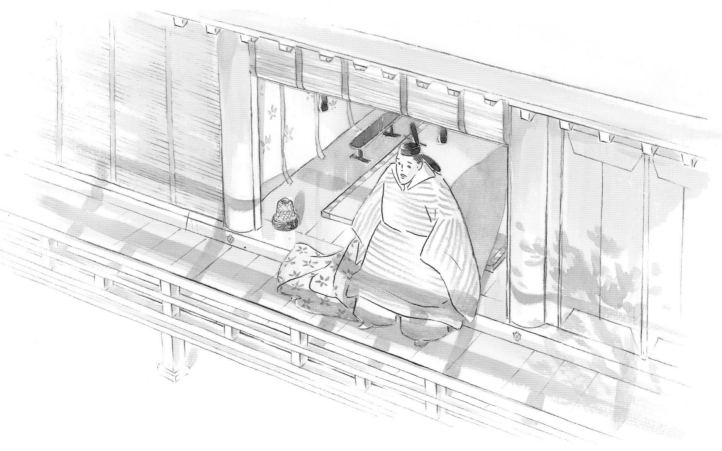

59/"Initially, I had the image of the moon being a world without color and only the earth looking blue. But it turned out that having some color was actually better, so I added the merest hint of pale purple here. The color is more restrained in the final film."

60/"As a general rule, we were not putting any color in the sky in this film, but when I was trying to get a feeling of summer, it felt lacking without those gigantic columns of clouds, so I put enough blue in the sky to make the white clouds visible."

59

60

61

62

61–64/"The mountains are a place of fond, happy memories for the princess. For all the work in this area, I had the art board as a base, so I was able to draw the background for the film itself relatively easily."

63

64

111

65

65/"The party coming from the moon rides a cloud. When I first drew this, I did so without thinking much about anything, but then I remembered a science fiction movie I'd seen a long time ago with a UFO in it. [*laughs*] This was back when I was still working at home, so even when I was drawing the actual background in the middle of the busiest part of production, I already had this image in my head, so I didn't have too rough a time with it."

66–69/"The last scene in the movie isn't just monotone or graytone. It might come across as monochromatic, but I didn't want to do something with one note. The truth is, when I was making the gray, I mixed in purples and cobalts and greens, so it ended up being this interesting color with little bits of those colors popping up somewhere from inside the gray. These were transparent watercolors, so having a little red stay in there was difficult, but using colors made in this way lets you feel the subtle changes in color, I think."

70–72/"I made roughly three types of colors and divided up the party that comes for the princess from the moon. If everyone in each shot is the same color, it looks monotonous, so I added colors ad hoc. For the clouds, the director of photography, Nakamura, put in a slightly subdued light, and I made a mottled paint for the shadows of the clouds and the king using a bright green, purple, and blue that weren't mixed too much. You can't tell just by looking at it, but I also had him do some processing so that the shadows were also moving." (See page 227.)

66

67

68

69

70

71

115

Background Arts Gallery

This section features backgrounds drawn by the art staff, led by Kazuo Oga, divided up into themes such as place and props. Some background images here have a separate foreground layered on them, while others have been processed digitally. The quoted comments are explanations from Kazuo Oga, while the text in square brackets contains the scene and sequence number from the film and the name of the artist who did the background. Images with no name listed were done by Kazuo Oga himself.

[S11-C21 background/Ayumi Kugawa]

1

Bamboo forest

1/The shining bamboo the bamboo cutter finds. [S1-C3]
2/The bamboo shoot sprouting up at the base. [S1-C6]
3/The shoot grows in the blink of an eye. An adorable girl is born from inside. [S1-C14/Katsu Hisamura]
4/The path through the bamboo forest the bamboo cutter walks to his house while carrying the girl. [S1-C33]
5/Shoots grow in the forest of timber bamboo. [S2D-C1]
6/The thicket of small bamboo where the young princess discovers the wild boar piglets. [S2D-C5 foreground cel on background]

"Takahata had the aim of having a light, rough art style for this entire film. Just like with the characters, I decided to not put too much shadow in the backgrounds and make it something of a level surface. But my own sensibility was that we might need a certain level of density and depth. For instance, with the individual bamboo stalks or the pillars in buildings, I didn't add enough depth to make them clearly cylindrical, but I worked with the way the light hits and the way I drew shadows to try and bring out a certain amount of roundness."

2

3

119

4

5

6

7

7/Bamboo forest bathed in evening sun. [S2D-C51]
8/Bamboo glowing as if to call out to the bamboo cutter. The light is white to indicate the connection with the moon. [S2D-C54]
9/Nuggets of gold pour out of where the bamboo cutter cuts the bamboo. [S2D-C61/Ayumi Kugawa]

8

9

10

11

12

10/Another bamboo stalk glows, and beautiful kimono come shooting out. [S3D-C1/Ayumi Kugawa]

11/Kimono shooting up high. The composition is the bamboo cutter looking up, and the sides are distorted like a video with a wide-angle lens. [S3D-C5/ Ayumi Kugawa]

12/The carriage that comes to take the princess and her family to the capital. Since there is an attendant carrying a torch, it's bright toward the back, while the forest in the front is drawn darker. [S4-C65]

1

The bamboo cutter's house

1/The full view of the bamboo cutter's house as seen from the yard. [S1-C52]
2/It's in a slightly higher place, with plum and magnolia trees. [S1-C53]
3/An early-spring scene with the buds of the plum tree starting to flower as i
mirroring the princess's growth. [S1-C87/Katsu Hisamura]
4/Rain in the rainy season. In the film, the princess plays happily outside th
house in the heavy rain. [S3A-C2]
5/The house bathed in reflected light when the princess comes home and learn
that they are setting out for the capital. [S4-C53]
6/The single path toward the carriage with the princess unable to even sa
goodbye to Sutemaru and the others. [S4-C62]
7/Her old home that the princess arrives at after flying out of her platform in th
capital. It already belongs to another family. There are still traces of the moon i
the early morning sky. [S8-C8/Yumi Hosaka]

2

3

4

5

6

7

8

9

10

8/The entrance and dirt-floor room of the bamboo cutter's house. [S1-C41]
9/The bamboo cutter and his wife work while letting the baby princess play on the straw mats. There is a weaver in the back. [S2B-C25/Takashi Kurahashi]
10/The walls are wood panels, while the floor is made of laid-out bamboo. [S2B-C19/Takashi Kurahashi]

1

Mountain scenes

1/The mountain road the bamboo cutter and his wife walk along when going to the wet nurse. [S1-C54]

2/The path through the woods that the bamboo cutter and his wife have walked countless times. [S1-C77]

3/On the bridge where the bamboo cutter's wife nurses the baby. In the film, the surface of the water is made to shimmer through a photographic effect. [S1-C64]

4/The magnolia tree rises up like a symbol of the princess's growth. The sky in the back and the tree were drawn separately and combined. Creating the white space for each and every one of the flowers opening from a bud required a lot of effort. [S2A-C7]

5/A bird's nest where the parent bird feeds its young. Drawn taking a cue from the paradise flycatcher, which makes its nest using bark. [S2C-C5]

6/Petals fallen from the snowbell onto the forest floor. [S2C-C8]

7/The grasses into which Sutemaru falls protecting the princess from the charging boar. [S2D-C16]

8/The children of the mountain appear carrying bamboo shoots. [S2D-C22]

9/The forest road that the princess, Sutemaru, and the children come down singing children's songs. In the movie, there is a squirrel in the branches above. [S2D-C32]

10/Along the road on the cliff. On the opposite side, a group of wisteria trees are blooming. [S2D-C38]

2

3

5

6

7

8

9

10

1

Lathe-turners' life

1/Rough bowls the lathe turners cut out. [S3A-C11/Tomotaka Kubo]
2/Inside Sutemaru's house. His father and older brother pour themselves into crafting bowls with their lathe. [S3A-C13/Takashi Kurahashi]
3/To the back is the hearth, while in front are the tools the mother uses to cut out the inside of the bowls. [S3A-C14/Takashi Kurahashi]

"We drew the lathe-turner settlement based on films and videos that recreated this life and work, and on books that discussed hidden villages. Apparently, there were several settlements like this around Kyoto, in particular in Shiga Prefecture. We had them make an appearance since the princess and her family would almost certainly have had contact with them. They show up only briefly, but I think the scenes of them working make an impression."

2

3

1

Summer

1/A waterfall in the mountains at the height of summer. A crested kingfisher rests on the branch in front. [S3B-C1]
2/The shallows the children play in. [S3B-C4]
3/Rock looking down on the river. The princess fearlessly jumps from here into the river. [S3B-C6]

"I went personally to Ohara in Kyoto to scout locations. There weren't any large rivers, but there were appropriate rocks, and I saw a river that was perfect for children to play in in the summer. There were also mountains, trees growing in the area, and grassy places where the princess and Sutemaru could run, so I was relieved. For the depiction of the plants growing on the mountain, I figured out what wasn't absolutely impossible; then I figured anything goes and I drew that. But of the summer grasses, there's a flower called red clover with a rich pink flower, and I drew this convenient plant since it would be an accent when I was drawing the field. But the crew told me that this was a naturalized plant and wasn't around in the Heian era, so I hurriedly erased it and corrected the image with a different flower. [*laughs*]"

2

3

4

4/The mountain road the children use to return home when they are done playing in the water. The columns of clouds and the summer sky are in the background, and the melon patch spreads out in front. [S3C-C1]

5/Summer mountains express the change of season with page 145-2 overlap. [S3E-C3]

6/Summer fields, overlap with page 145-3. The akebia fruit is still green. [S3E-C2]

5

6

1

Fall

1/Lathe-turner settlement welcoming the fall coloring the trees. [S3E-C4]
2/Fall mountains overlapping from page 142-5. [S3E-C3]
3/Fall fields overlapping from page 142-6. [S3E-C2]

"I drew the large dead tree in the lathe-turner settlement as a marker to understand that we were in the same place even with the seasonal changes. In the latter half, the princess comes here after Sutemaru and the others have moved on and the settlement is gone. I wanted to make one thing that was familiar, given that the look of the place would change with the withering of winter or the summer grasses of her reunion with Sutemaru. Because with this tree, it wasn't just the princess but also the viewers who would know that this was a place of memories. At first, I made it a fir tree or a white pine, some kind of coniferous tree with leaves, but drawing the dead tree felt clean and easy to understand, so I changed it to its current form."

2

3

4

5

6

4/The exterior of the lathe turners' house. It's adorned with a talisman against evil spirits made of animal bones. [S3E-C5/Tatsuya Kushida]
5/The forest where the children find the pheasant. [S4-C5]
6/The mountain grape tree the children climb to pick the fruit. [S3E-C11]

7/The mountain path that the children walk home on in the evening sun carrying the pheasant they caught and the mountain vegetables they picked. [S4-C50]

Winter

1/The hometown road that the princess comes back on in a daze. The dawn is near. [S8-C1]
2/The remains of the lathe-turner settlement the princess comes to. The only thing to indicate that Sutemaru and the others were there is the dead tree. [S8-C19]
3/The charcoal-making hut in the woods where the princess meets the old man. [S8-C14]
4/The fields in snow after time has passed since 1. [S8-C35 foreground cel on background]

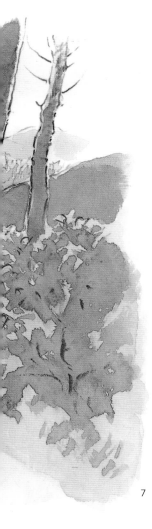

7

1

2

4

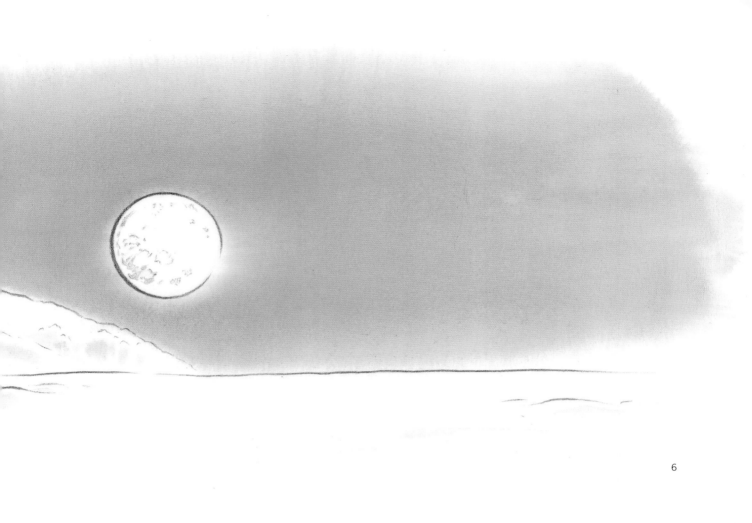

6

5/The snowy scene where the princess collapses after losing everything. [S8-C39]
6/The moon looking down on the despairing princess. Is this a momentary dream or reality? [S8-C36]

5

1

2

Trees, flowers, and fruit

1/Plum blossoms beginning to unfold. [S1-C81]
2/Magnolia tree with buds opening. [S2A-C6]
3/New buds sprouting in the new spring. [S2C-C2/Katsu Hisamura]
4/Vividly colored wisteria flowers. [S2C-C3/Satoko Nakamura]
5/Rhododendron. [S2C-C4/Shiho Sato]
6/Plums harvested in a break from the rain. [S3A-C5]

3

4

5

6

7

8

9

12

13

14

7/Shepherd's purse rocked in the wind. [S11-C6/Katsu Hisamura]
8/Horsetail. [S11-C5/Katsu Hisamura]
9/Chinese milk vetch. [S11-C4/Katsu Hisamura]
10/A brown cicada announcing the summer. [S3B-C10]
11/Ginger growing near the lathe turners' home. [S16A-C43]
12/The melon patch the princess unthinkingly steals from. [S3C-C2]
13/Mountain grape branches heavy with fruit. [S3E-C12/Shiho Sato]
14/The basket left behind by the princess when she leaves for the capital. It's full of mountain grapes, oyster mushrooms, and the other food she gathered that day. [S4-C64]

1

The court at the capital

1/The mansion the bamboo cutter builds in the capital to try and make the princess, a gift from the heavens, into a real princess. There is a building to the side over the pond in the tradition style. [S5-C47/Tomotaka Kubo]

2/The main building where guests are received and the covered path connecting the ends of the house. [S5-C16/Tomotaka Kubo]

3/The inner courtyard where the craftsmen come to get payment for the jeweled branch from Mount Horai Prince Kuramochi brings. [S13A-C75/Takashi Kurahashi]

4/The interior closed room where clothing and accessories are kept. The princess is delighted to see the beautiful kimono. [S5-C30]

5/The inside of the closed room seen from the back of the room. [S5-C35]

6/The hallway the princess runs around in, overjoyed by the kimono. [S5-C44/Tomotaka Kubo]

7/The central room where Lady Sagami, the princess's tutor, spreads out the picture scroll to show her. The scroll was drawn separately on a foreground. [S6-C5/Yumi Hosaka]

"For the kimono that the princess sees for the first time in the capital (pages 162–64), I put plenty of water on the paper, and then I rolled a roll of toilet paper on top of that to clear away just the water on the surface. Doing this before painting leaves behind a slight pattern when the water dries. I used this method with the idea that it could look like the texture of the kimono fabric. Toilet paper is a very useful tool for art. [laughs] Here, we put another transparent cel on top and drew the patterns in white."

2

3

4

5

6

7

Life in the capital

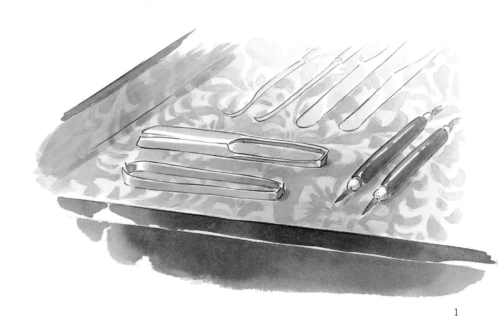

1

2

3

4

5

6

1/The princess's makeup tools. Brushes to apply tooth-blackening dye, tweezers, a razor, a brow pencil, a comb, scissors, a bowl with handles, and other items are laid out. [S7-C5/Takashi Kurahashi]
2/Same. [S7-C3/Takashi Kurahashi]
3/Same. [S7-C4/Takashi Kurahashi]
4/Doodles the princess does during her study time. The picture is a collage of those drawn in the animation. [S6-C13/Katsu Hisamura]
5/The matching clams the princess plays with when she's bored. [S8-C45 foreground cel on background/Tomotaka Kubo]
6/Me no Warawa dipping the brush for princess's tooth blackening. [S9-C7 foreground cel on background]

1

2

3

Darkness

1/The night of the banquet for the princess's coming of age. The doors she pushes away in her anger at the heartless words of the guests. [S7-C75]
2/ Same. Wooden walls of the hallway. [S7-C76]
3/Same. The house gates. [S7-C77]
4/The main road the princess runs down while tearing off her skirt. [S7-C78B]
5/The mountain road where the exhausted princess falls. [S7-C84/Yohei Takamatsu]

4

5

The princess's quarters

1

1/The princess's quarters and sleeping area. In the actual film, there is a pillar in front and a screen placed behind as a kind of partition that flutters in the breeze. [S13A-C3/Tomotaka Kubo]
2/The platform where the princess usually sits. A koto and an armrest are set out. [S13D-C7]
3/The room facing the inner courtyard where the princess rejects the mikado's wooing. The front facing the yard is bright and the shadows are red. The shadows deeper into the room are emphasized. [S14-C58/Takashi Kurahashi]
4/Same. Bird's-eye view. [S14-C61/Takashi Kurahashi]

1

Outbuilding and garden

1/The hallway leading to the outbuilding where the bamboo cutter's wife and the princess spend a lot o
time. [S6-C50]

2/Inside the outbuilding, which has the same construction as a mountain house. There is a loom wher
the bamboo cutter's wife weaves and the princess's kimono are hung neatly on either side. [S6-C35]

3/Wooden floor, dirt floor, hearth. For the princess, this is a comforting place to spend time with th
bamboo cutter's wife. [S6-C52]

4/The loom, forgotten at some point with the changes in the princess's heart, covered in spider web
from disuse. It is illuminated by the white light of the moon. [S15-C7]

5/One corner of the artificial hill the princess made because she missed her mountain life. A hut ar
waterwheel are set in the midst of the grasses, creating a scene like her mountain home. [S13E-C10]

6/The inner courtyard, bathed in moonlight, where the princess is in anguish. [S13E-C29]

2

3

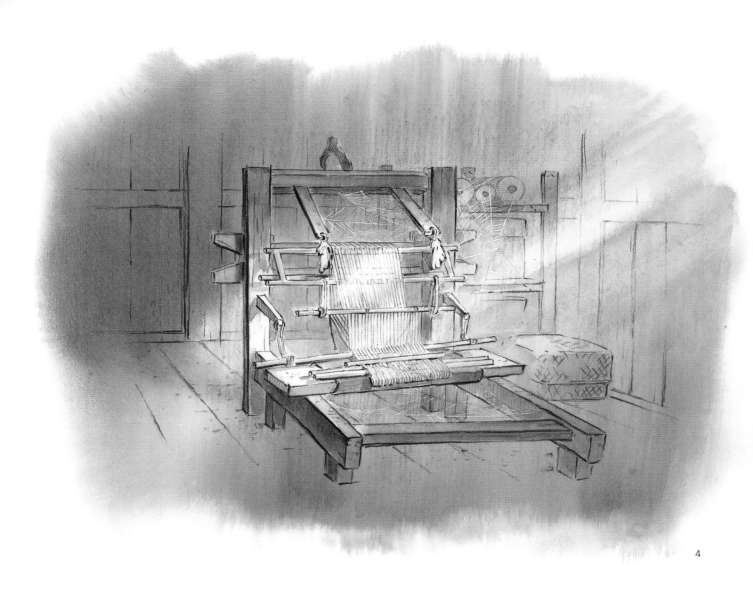

4

5

6

Mountain sakura

2

1/The mountain scene where they go to have a flower-viewing party after the princess invites the bamboo cutter's wife and Me no Warawa. The princess jumps down from the carriage and runs up the mountain path toward the large sakura tree. [S11-C10]
2/The colors of spring are still sparse on the mountain they visit in the carriage. [S11-C1]
3/Same. The mountain is colored with sakura seen from the carriage. [S11-C8]
4/The mountain path the princess runs up happy like a child. [S11-C12/Katsu Hisamura]
5/The large sakura tree in full bloom at the top of the hill. [S11-C15]

3

4

Seiryoden

1/The magnificent Seiryoden, where the mikado lives. [S14-C1/Takashi Kurahashi]
2/The mikado's room at Seiryoden. Scrolls with Chinese poems on them hang here. [S14-C26/Takashi Kurahashi]
3/The carriage porch at the bamboo cutter's house. The mikado is inside, having heard the rumors about the princess. [S14-C29]

2

3

Legend of the Heavenly Maiden

1/The scene drawn while the princess sings "Song of the Heavenly Maiden." Mt. Fuji can be seen with a trail of smoke in the distance. [S16A-C16]

2/Same. The shore where, having been left behind, the father and child think of the maiden and look up at the moon. [S16A-C18]

186

1

2

1

Reunion

1/The mountain road the princess parts the summer grasses to walk up. [S16A-C39 foreground cel on background]
2/A place of fond memories from the princess's childhood that she visits once more. [S16A-C38]
3/The pass where the lathe turners rest, with Sutemaru's family in the lead. [S16B-C1]

2

3

Flight

1

2

1/Bird's-eye view of the paradise-like field of flowers that the princess and Sutemaru fly over. [S16C-C10]
2/Same. A field of rice glittering a golden yellow in autumn. [S16C-C14]
3/The pair joyously ascend the large tree that is actually a guardian deity. [S16C-C16]
4/The beautiful, peaceful mountain scene they look down on. [S16C-C18]
5/A tranquil sea they fly past. [S16C-C19 foreground cel on background]
6/The moon in the middle of the day shining white. Their joy is fleeting; the power of the moon rips them apart. [S16C-C20]
7/The ocean jetting a pillar of water when the princess falls. [S16C-C19]

"In old Japanese paintings, especially in picture scrolls, the sky is basically not drawn. At most, there are drifting clouds, and the sky and the ground are generally the same color. So by simplifying drawing the lines and adding color to people and the main areas, you come to see something like a sky. But since the rest of the picture looks strange if you add color to only the sky in the depths of the image and nowhere else, the blank space that is the point of this film won't be realized. Thus, except for the summer clouds in the scene where the children are at the melon patch, I basically drew no blue skies. But then in the end comes the scene where the princess and Sutemaru are flying. Once they take off from the ground, there's nothing to draw but the sky. [*laughs*] For the sake of this scene when the princess truly feels the wonder of the earth, Takahata said we dared not to draw the sky before, so here I did the blue of the sky a bit on the heavy side."

4

6

7

1

The moon

1/The full moon shining above the rear courtyard. It watches over the princess as she destroys the hill she made in a fit of violent emotion. [S13E-C28]

2/The moon as seen from the pool house. The night of the full moon when they come for her draws near. [S15-C1]

3/The house that Sutemaru and his wife are roofing the night the princess leaves for the moon. [S17-C113]

4/The pool house where the princess sinks into sadness because she doesn't want to go back to the moon. [S15-C2]

5/Bird's-eye view of the house the party of the moon king descends on, riding clouds. This is the first time the entire scene was drawn. [S17-C1/Tomotaka Kubo]

6/The moon of the fifteenth night that gets larger as the party approaches, and the watchtower where the warriors lie in wait. [S17-C105/Tomotaka Kubo]

7/The settlement of Sutemaru and the lathe turners being rebuilt. [S17-C109]

8/The moon the princess returns to. [S17-C118]

2

3

197

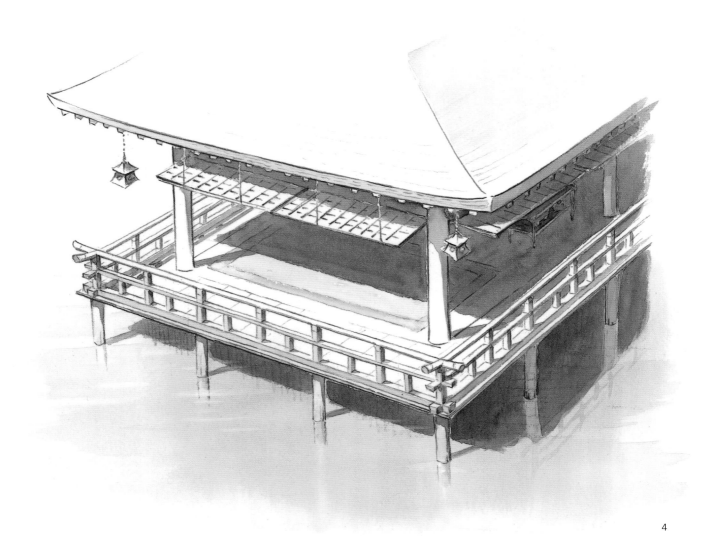

4

5

6

9/The earth the princess suddenly turns to look at after losing all her memories and returning to the moon. [S17-C122]

"Rather than the earth as seen from space that we're used to in photos from NASA, Takahata put in a difficult order: the earth as it would have been imagined in the Heian era when no one had seen it yet. But when I tried, it ended up being that familiar blue earth and the swirling clouds, and no matter how many times I redid it, I couldn't get the go-ahead from him. Eventually, I tried making the picture of the small Earth I drew in the scene where the angel from the moon appears. This was at the stage where the movie was very nearly complete, but I finally got him to accept it and go with this one. This was actually the last sequence for the art department work."

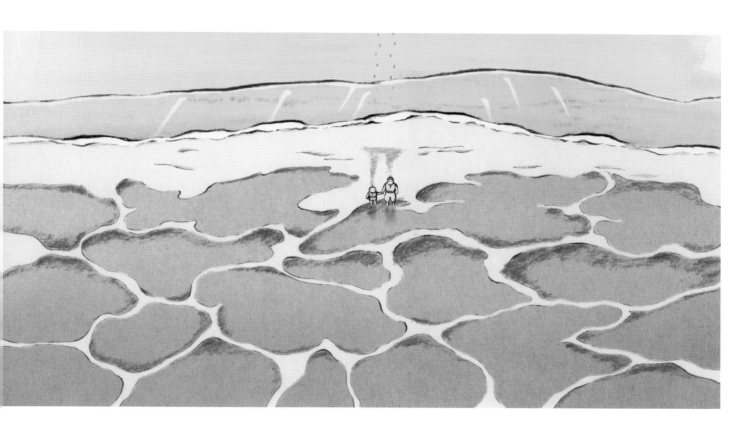

Cinematic Expression

This section focuses on photography techniques in the process that comes after the animation and art that have been discussed so far, and on how *The Tale of the Princess Kaguya* was made and what kind of creative tricks were used for each sequence.

One Sequence Start to Finish

The sequence we look at here is [S13A-C5 key animations/Masashi Ando, background/ Tomotaka Kubo]. It tells of how "three years went by" and shows the bamboo cutter's wife at the loom and the princess winding thread in the guest house. Learn how the work progressed and the processes that take it from storyboard to completed sequence.

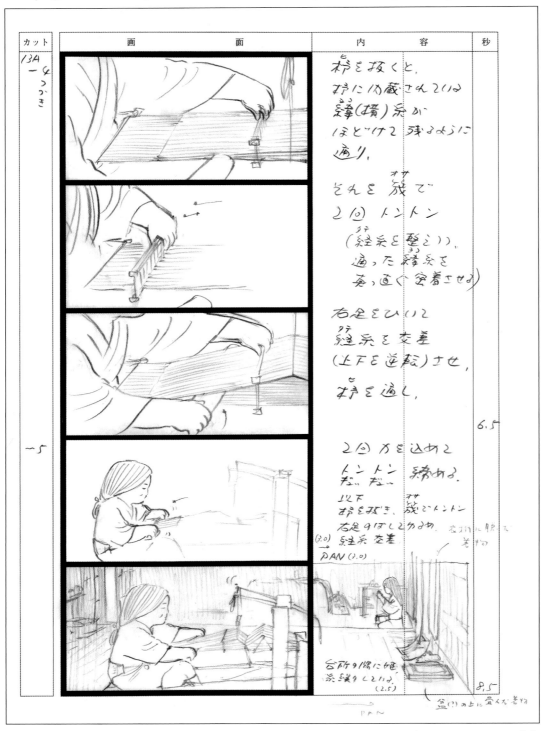

To produce this sequence, it was necessary to carefully draw the operation of the loom. To that end, the staff checked all kinds of references and went to talk to Bryan Whitehead, a Canadian expert in ancient Japanese looms.

1. Script, storyboard

The preliminary script says, "As sunlight pours in through the open side door and skylight, the bamboo cutter's wife is weaving. On the straw mats pulled onto the dirt floor that leads from the kitchen, the princess sits in work clothes, winding thread. Around them are shelves with matching clams, dolls, and piles of pamphlets, and we can see how they are comfortable in this place." The storyboard is created based on this script.

Sometimes, Osamu Tanabe makes the film storyboard to be used for the animation based on Takahata's plan, while other times, other staff members (Shinsaku Sasaki, Masako Sato, and Shinji Hashimoto) make the rough storyboard based on Takahata's plan and Tanabe goes on to make that the animation storyboard. For scenes 16 and 17, Yoshiyuki Momose created the storyboard based on Takahata's plan. Shinsaku Sasaki was responsible for the rough storyboard for this sequence (below). Osamu Tanabe did the animation storyboard.

Rough storyboard by Shinsaku Sasaki.

S13A-C5 layout. Layouts are generally drawn by the animator for that sequence (Masashi Ando in this case), checked by directing animator Osamu Tanabe, and then passed on to animation and art.

S13A-C5 art board. The art boards for the film was done by Kazuo Oga. Normally, the art director creates a rough image of the background, called the production imageboard, and shares this with the director and staff before drawing the actual background. For the film, art board with the characters is drawn as in the above. The role of the production imageboard is of course to unify the characters and the background, and the staff use the art board to examine the coloring of the characters and the unpainted areas.

2. Layout, concept sketch

The role of the layout and concept sketch is to decide how to create the actual screen in line with the completed storyboard. In Hayao Miyazaki's works, the imageboard is drawn freely, imaging the characters and scenes before starting the storyboard, while the concept sketch is drawn after the scene structures are decided in the storyboard and the layouts to examine how to depict these scenes.

1

2

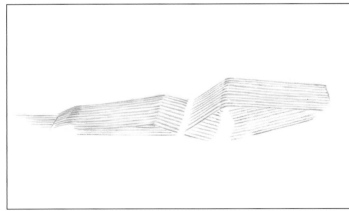

4

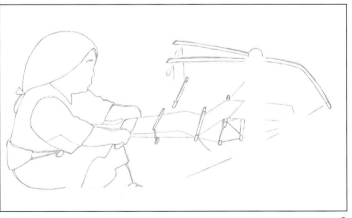

3

5

6

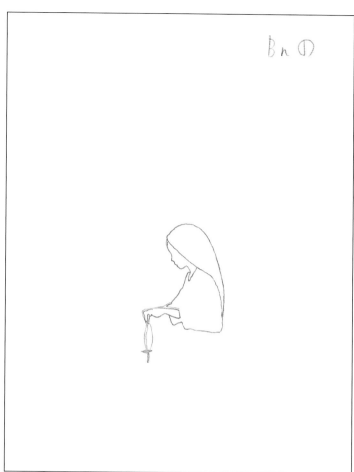

8

7

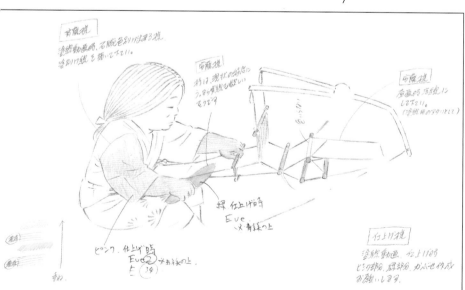

9

3. Animation

Animating movement (key animation drawing and in-betweens) is done based on the layouts. The strength of this film is that the character lines are not all as uniform as possible; rather, the artists make use of the pencil line and its differing weights. There are also the color lines that indicate the areas to be colored and left uncolored inside the character lines, and the pattern lines that express the patterns on kimonos and other things, which are all drawn on their own separate pages. The key animations are drawn by the animator in charge of the scene, checked by supervising animator Osamu Tanabe, and then given a final detailed revision by animation supervisor Kenichi Konishi. The animation for color and design lines is done by Masaya Saito and a few others, and the animation is completed through in-betweens and motion checks.

Images 1–8 on this page are only one part of the animation elements created for S13A-C5:
1/The layout revision to determine the placement of the characters within the sequence.
2/The key animation and texture animations for the bamboo cutter's wife at the front.
3/The paint outlines.
4/The texture animations for the loom. (The pattern is complicated, so it's drawn on a separate page.)
5/The mask indicator to paste the wooden background material for the loom.
6/The key animation of the princess toward the back.
7/ It was drawn as a still image of her lower half, which doesn't move (including texture animations).
8/The paint outlines for her upper body.
9/A collection of notes written by a directorial assistant for the animators and ink and paint staff in drawing this sequence.

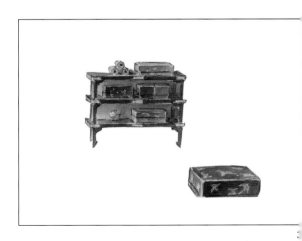

4. Art

1 is the background drawing the art director redrew after making adjustments to the lines in order to draw the actual background based on the layout on page 205. 2 is the background image colored in watercolors based on that original drawing. 3 is the foreground redrawn in parts. When there are these kinds of drawn additions, or when characters are between two backgrounds, or, in the case where there is complicated camera work, the image is sometimes made of several parts set on the main background according to the composition of the screen; these parts are called foregrounds.

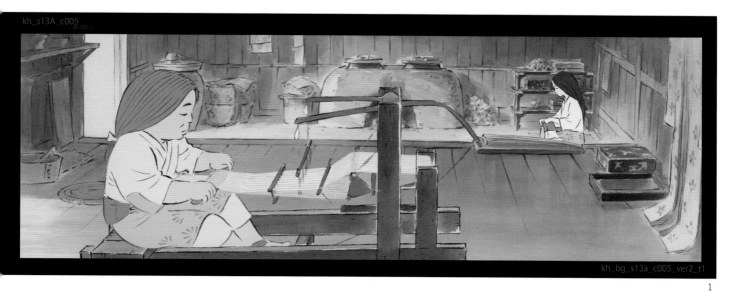

kh_s13A_c005

kh_bg_s13a_c005_ver2_t1

1

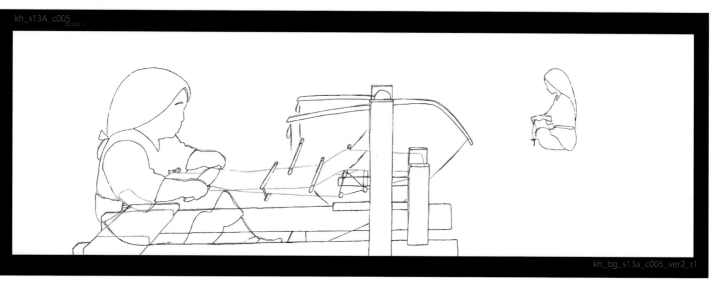

kh_s13A_c005

kh_bg_s13a_c005_ver2_t1

2

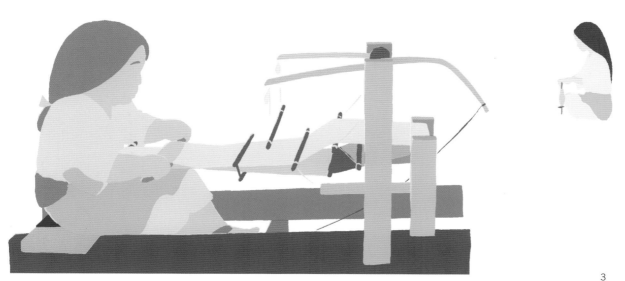

3

5. Color board

The key for coloring is selected from the key animations drawn for the animation on pages 206 and 207 and scanned. At this point, there is no animation of the paint outlines, and color setter Yukiko Kakita considers the coloring and blank spaces with art director Kazuo Oga's art board as the model (page 205-2) before coloring on the computer. What is actually placed on top of the background in the movie is the color board in 1. Takahata and the rest of the main staff check this and look for the approach to line quality, a sense of unity with the character coloring and background, and the way of drawing blank spaces. Based on the decision here, work on the color animation proceeds. Additionally, depending on the sequence, they may return to the key frames or artwork and make corrections. 2 is the paint outline animation based on this color board. 3 is the colored image finished in paint outline animation drawing.

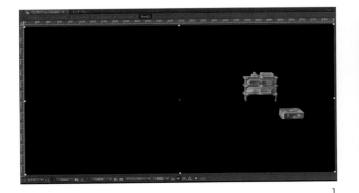

1

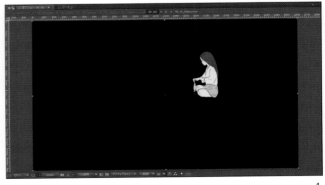

4

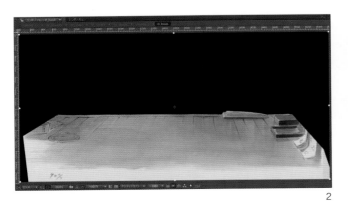

2

5

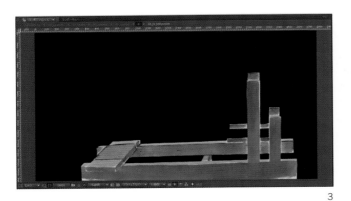

3

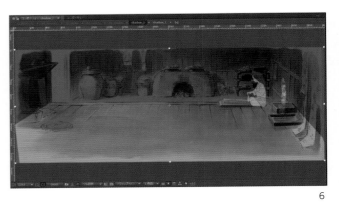

6

Here we have some of the digital images from photography for S13A-C5. It isn't an especially difficult sequence, but it does have elements of a certain level of detail layered to create the film. 1–3 are some of the foreground elements. The shelves with the scrolls behind the princess and the box next to the kimono were changed slightly and handled as foregrounds. For the loom in front, after a mask was created in finishing, the rough wood texture was pasted in as a foreground element.

4–6 are some of the princess elements. The shadow to the right behind the princess also moves slightly in line with her movement, but since this shadow was a little unnatural, a semitransparent element was made and color irregularities were added so that it would blend in with the wooden wall of the background.

6. Photography to completion

All of the elements drawn thus far are digitized, and the film takes shape under the eyes of the director of photography. Photography is not simply a matter of putting the elements together; the camera movement and the flow of time that determine the tone of the film must be decided on, and transparency, light, smoke, and other special effects, along with 3D graphics in recent years, must be incorporated into the film naturally. The job here is to pull out the meaning of the shot and produce a final form for the screen on a level that the director and the rest of the staff approve of. Because photography is the last process in making a film, it's a difficult department that bears the fallout of delays in other processes, but at the same time, it could also be said to be the last stand to make the film even better.

7

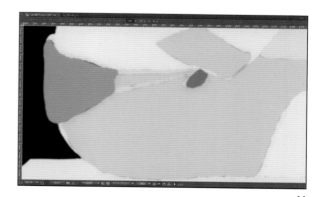

11

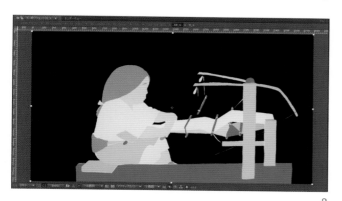

8

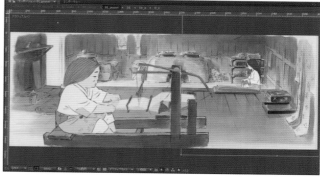

12

9

13

10

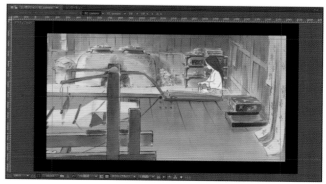

14

7–10 are some of the bamboo cutter's wife elements: 7 incorporates the actual linework, 8 has the color lines colored, and 9 has the pattern lines colored, and 10 is a mask element of the finished character element for adjusting the saturation to make it blend more seamlessly into the background by adding some irregularity.

11–14 are the final steps in the photography process: 11 is added ink spread, which mitigates the uniform digital elements by adding some bleed to the edges of the paint outlines to make them fit in with the background better. 12 is the overall look of the completed image. 13 and 14 are camera instructions. These indicate the start and stop points of the camera moving from left to right.

Director of Digital Imaging
Keisuke Nakamura

"There was a lot of trial and error, a number of retakes, but the redoing itself was fun work."

Keisuke Nakamura: Born July 1969 in Nagasaki prefecture. While still a student at Musashino Art University studying oil painting, he was employed as a CG designer at Ludens. He joined T2studio in 2001. He was a part of the production of the Studio Ghibli film *The Cat Returns* (2002) as a CG animator. He made his debut as a director of photography on the TV series *Phoenix* (2004). As a CG designer, he worked on the feature-length animated film *Steamboy* (2004) and the OVA *Diebuster* (2004–2006). In recent years, he has been the director of digital imaging for the TV series *Genji Monogatari Sennenki: Genji* (2009), *Steins;Gate* (2011), and the film *Magic Tree House* (2012), among others. He began work on *The Tale of the Princess Kaguya* as the director of digital imaging for the 2011 pilot film.

Digital imaging for *The Tale of the Princess Kaguya* was outsourced to T2studio, and Keisuke Nakamura, who came up as a CG designer, took the role of director of digital imaging. He has worked on 3D graphics in film and for TV. What was it like to work on a Ghibli film in a major role as the director of digital imaging with a deep knowledge of digital work, and what was it like on the frontlines of a work directed by Isao Takahata? He talks about the cinematic expression born of the combination of performance, animation, and art from the perspective of digital imaging.

The last Studio Ghibli film you worked on was *The Cat Returns*, right?

Nakamura: That's right. The former president of T2studio, Hirokata Takahashi, knew Takahata and Hayao Miyazaki from their days at Toei. After the company made the shift to digital, I had the help of Kakita [Yukiko], who was with me on this one as well as the color setter. I had that experience, and then T2studio was asked to do the photography and processing for this film, too. I just happened to be working on the historical anime *Genji Monogatari Sennenki: Genji*, which deals with the Heian era, and this was a film where the work was expected to continue steadily over a long period, so Kentaro Takahashi (the current president) thought that I might be suited to it, and I ended up being put in charge of the project.

This was my first time on a Takahata film and my first time properly involved in a Studio Ghibli film as the director of digital imaging. Since a photography director I really admire at Ghibli, Atsushi Okui, was also there, I was incredibly nervous at first. Then Okui said to me that I should just do the work the way I always do, and I felt like I could relax a little and get started with the work. [*laughs*]

Did you start from the making of the pilot film?

Nakamura: That is where our work began. Actually, before I started at T2studio, I spent about a year at Studio Ghibli laying the groundwork. But at that point, the direction was basically set, and it ended up that we would put what we had onto film and then everyone, including the director, would have a look at it.

As for Takahata, he wanted to make a film that was different from *My Neighbors the Yamadas*. He again wanted to make use of Osamu Tanabe's abilities, but he said that he wasn't simply looking for watercolor art. So then what specifically did he want to change? What would be good to change? Rather than a straightforward, clear instruction, this took the form of searching and questioning for a while at the pilot-film stage. We built up ideas by looking at the finished art one piece at a time and discussing those images.

At first, we considered all kinds of things, like what kind of effects to put on the art Tanabe had drawn, whether we could match them well with Oga's backgrounds, or if it might be better not to match them too closely. We went through a lot of trial and error. When we watched the completed film, we knew only too well everything that had changed over the course of production: what was finished near the beginning and what was made after a little time had passed. The overall style and tone didn't change significantly, so I don't think your average viewer would really be able to tell.

For this film, both the animation and the art were based on Tanabe's images, and the task at hand was the rather large objective of bringing out the flavor of the lines he drew in pencil and brushwork. What was your awareness of this?

Nakamura: Bringing out the quality of the linework as much as possible was the thing we were all concerned with, including Kakita in ink and paint. As a result, we had all kinds of situations and conditions. There were times when things just wouldn't go according to plan. But I heard all the animators were trying all sorts of things with line quality, too. They hung on right until the very end, and Tanabe and supervising animator Kenichi Konishi revised by hand the lines of a hundred sequences in the digital format. Oga was also concerned about the way the blank spaces looked, and he repainted about four hundred sequences, including backgrounds, focusing on the coloring and on places that were too heavy or too faint.

I saw this common ground at an earlier stage as the point of combining Tanabe's art style, Oga's backgrounds, and Takahata's direction. It had always been Takahata's intention to not tweak the images and ruin the hand-drawn feeling, and in that sense, I think we managed to finish it up without moving too far from that original vision. For us, the tools were digital, but we tried to support from behind the scenes while trying to use the hand-drawn elements to their ultimate potential.

As the director of photography, what was the thing you kept in mind most of all for this film?

Nakamura: It's gotten harder to keep traces of the hand-drawn nuance in animation nowadays, but for *The Tale of the Princess Kaguya*, I incorporated as many of the things drawn on paper as I could. I put these on the screen without making them too clean, so inevitably, there were going to be places where it wasn't going to all come together on its own. To avoid that, from the ink and paint stage, we were including things like cutting and pasting for every sequence, adjusting on a very fine scale to make something slightly darker or lighter, doing each and every adjustment so that it wouldn't be conspicuous. This took an incredible amount of work.

This is both an advantage and a disadvantage of working digitally: on a computer, you can process and create an image with clean elements and zero static. But the backgrounds that Oga and the other artists did had the grain of the page and other variations. Of course, the key animations drawn by the animators were also on paper, but since these end up perfectly immaculate after the processes of ink and paint, to get closer to both, we added a light paper texture, carefully balancing all the elements, for all the cels.

We also added effects to produce a sense of irregularity to a lot of the sequences, including the backgrounds. But we couldn't end up with any discontinuity because of these effects, so getting that balance was difficult. It was a subtle effect for each of the different elements, but the staff worked hard to make things look as much as possible like a single picture on the screen.

So then what gave you the most trouble in the photography of *The Tale of the Princess Kaguya*?
Nakamura: This is not so much me, but what made Kakita rack her brain in the ink and paint stage before us was that for a lot of scenes, Takahata and Tanabe were both fixated on "white," which resulted in redoing a lot of things. There was also this theory of making use of the blank spaces on the screen. In terms of performances, it would be to express the princess's feelings, some symbolism, or because they wanted to bring out the colors in the kimono—there were all kinds of reasons, but this was different from the white in a normal anime. In the end, the white of the background-art page became the standard, so we needed to adjust the digital white to match that.

Naturally, we followed up in photography, but the coloring issue was especially difficult when the digital and analog elements were mixed. At Studio Ghibli, we don't scan the background art; we photograph it with a digital camera and then load it into the computer. We struggled with the coloring here. It would end up yellowish or bluish, or we just couldn't see the white at all, or there'd be the "white color" where there were subtle differences even in the same white. We kept making adjustments in photography right up until the end.

We photographed the background art with a digital camera again for this film. To make animation these days, you usually use a scanner to read and digitize the images, but with a scanner, the light source and the subject are too close together, so some people are of the opinion that the scanned image is inevitably too heavy. If you use a camera, I think things like the mood and depth come out more naturally in an image, maybe because you have some space in between the art and the camera. You might end up seeing a lot of the paper quality, which does not work with every style of the film, so you can't simply say that one way is good and the other is bad. But the policy at Studio Ghibli of photographing background art with a camera has real meaning, and I think it was especially appropriate for this film.

Also, at the preparation stage, the methods were originally set out into three types of drawing: paint outlines, principal lines, and texture animations. This is also what we did on *My Neighbors*, but a lot of people on the floor were saying that the burden on the animators was too great and this was just too difficult. So then maybe we could drop it down to two types of hand-drawn lines, meaning we skip the paint outlines and make the thick coloring happen from the principal lines—this was the initial expectation of digital production, including the photography process. But even if a simple silhouette

would have been fine, it would be extremely difficult to place the lines to differentiate color close to the principal lines for inner lines like eyes, noses, mouths, and kimono. To be more efficient, we gave up on this in the end. That said, this film always had a vast number of frames, so we did want to help the animators if we could, and we tried to take on as much of the processing with different elements and methods as we could.

Was this an independent determination by you and the digital imaging team?
Nakamura: Takahata and supervising animator Keisuke Nakamura both asked me to take care of the trace and shift (creating a subtle blur by sliding each panel of the animation very slightly, even for sequences where the characters don't move) and the reflections in photography.

Trace and shift is an animation technique, so in general, the animators create this by hand, but this time the movement that was difficult to draw was left to photography. I'm sure you've seen a video where the character is just flapping their mouth and their body doesn't move at all. We didn't leave them like that in this film, though. When mouths were moving or hands were gesturing, we added movement and made the rough surfaces move to the extent it was possible in photography so that it looks like some part of their body is always moving.

Also, the reflections of characters in the wooden floors of the buildings were all done by photography. (See page 217.) Both of these are fairly straightforward jobs, but they go on at length throughout the film, so these two were places where photography put in particular effort.

For this kind of practical work, I had more conversations with Tanabe and Keisuke Nakamura. Tanabe in particular was always taking the lead with the visuals, and he gave us all kinds of images. We did the work by fiddling with things in response and handing them back.

This straightforward work supporting the team behind the scenes went on for a long time. When you look back now, how was this job on *The Tale of the Princess Kaguya*?
Nakamura: I've talked about this a lot with the staff I worked with. We tried so many different kinds of things. I think that if we were to make another movie using these methods, given that we've already sorted it all out—for photography at least—we could probably put together a more effective way of doing it.

And I'm normally in an office with nothing but photography staff. Going into a studio full of people from animation, art, and other departments and being able to work with the director the whole time was great. Everyone involved is the cream of the crop when it comes to animation in Japan. It was incredible seeing Takahata carefully check each and every sequence and give instructions to adjust the timing on the level of individual frames.

When we saw the film after ink and paint, there was a ton of revision work to be done, and the photography staff persevered and stuck with me right up until the end. Within myself, I had an awareness of these revisions as also being a part of the process. I think maybe Takahata had the strong desire to try with digital the things he couldn't do back in the cel animation days. It was a huge experience to be able to see him doing this up close. So while it's worth celebrating that it's finished now, I also have this feeling I don't know how to describe. A bit sad that it's over. Tanabe said the same thing. I think it really was a great place to work.

Cinematic Expression 1
Fabric textures

[S2B-C2 key animation/Takayuki Hamada, background/Kazuo Oga]

1

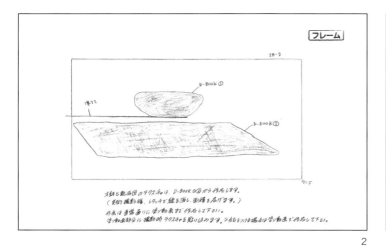

2

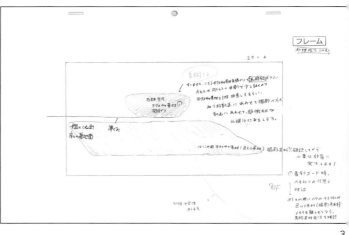

3

1/Art board by Kazuo Oga. This piece was the guiding image for the texture and blank space for the blanket that the baby lies on and the kimono laid on top of her.

2, 3/Notes on how to express the texture of the blanket and the stone bowl next to it. To express textures when applying color variation after ink and paint processes, the image produced by the art staff is incorporated, and a variety of methods are employed depending on the content of the sequence, such as pasting elements into each panel.

4

5

8

6

9

7

4 is the background for S2B-C2. 5–9 are completed images. When the baby moves, the blankets and clothing move with her. The stone bowl the bamboo cutter's wife is using to knead soba is the same.

"I think that if you looked at this normally, you wouldn't notice anything, but that's good. As a trick to express a subtle flavor, we added a varied texture, the artistic effect of paper, to the foreground cel parts that are not background. I did all the sequences by pasting textures on the finished cel or adding variation like bleed."

(Keisuke Nakamura, director of digital imaging. All comments below are also his.)

Cinematic Expression 2
Kimono patterns
[S5–C30 key animation/Norio Matsumoto, background/Kazuo Oga]

1

2

4

3

2–4 are the completed images for the scene where the princess touches the kimono, lifts it up, and plays with it. As the background, the kimono was drawn as if it's moving, but the white pattern was drawn one page at a time in animation, and the variation in the red is expressed by incorporating the texture of the kimono drawn in the background of 1 by one of the art staff.

"We incorporated the background Oga did and changed the shape in photography to match the shape of the kimono changing in animation. This isn't the result of CG or anything like that—it's just straightforward work by hand."

Cinematic Expression 3
Reflections in the floor
[S5–C11, S5–C56 key animation/Norio Matsumoto, background/Tomotaka Kubo]

1

5

2

6

3

7

4

The floors of the palatial Heian mansion they move into in the capital are beautifully polished and show reflections. 1–7 above are all completed images, and the reflections move together with the characters' movement. There's also no sense of the shadows of the pillars in the background being out of place. The majority of these were added during photography.

"The basic concept is mirror reflection, where we process and use the reflection of the animated picture as if in a mirror. But for those scenes when we can't do that, when someone is crawling for instance, we make mask elements in photography and bring the reflection effect about like that. Each reflection is not such difficult work on its own, but these scenes are particularly hard for the staff as they need to add shadows of reflections to everything in the room."

Cinematic Expression 4
Expressing hair

[S2B-C13 key animation/Takayuki Hamada], [S16C-C26 key animation/Shinji Hashimoto]

1

2

3

4

5

6

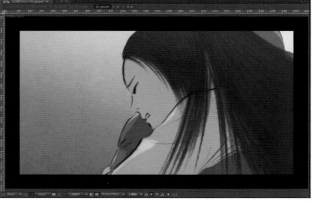

7

1–3 are selections of what the staff were instructed to do to process the hair for the baby princess. 4–7 are photography process images for S16C-C26. For the grown-up princess's hair, parts were drawn as texture animations to add to the principal lines and the paint outlines; then a soft texture was added. Not all sequences are processed like this, but this sort of method is used to emphasize the texture of the hair.

"We add a haziness to the hairline for a lot of characters. For the grown princess's hair, these pattern lines were added to the ends of her hair in animation, and I think it's effective in giving a sense of depth without being too much. Well, I suppose it's like a wig or a hairpiece then. [*laughs*]"

Cinematic Expression 5
Panning camerawork
[S5-C18 key animation/Norio Matsumoto, background/Tomotaka Kubo]

1

5

2

6

3

7

4

1–7 are the completed images for S5-C18. This shot has the bamboo cutter and his wife in the field of view like traditional hina dolls while we get a wraparound of the princess's appearance after arriving at the mansion in the capital. This looks like 3D computer graphics, but it's actually a sequence created with a lot of labor on normal panning camerawork.

"For the sense of motion, it might look like we used 3D software, but the background is a still image. We moved the size of the pillars and floor in front like stretching an elastic to depict a loose wraparound. The platform and folding screen behind the pillars were moved using a quasi-3D. But this method took far too much work, so it wasn't used heavily."

Camera work

[S11C-C20 key animation/Shinji Hashimoto, background/Ayumi Kugawa]

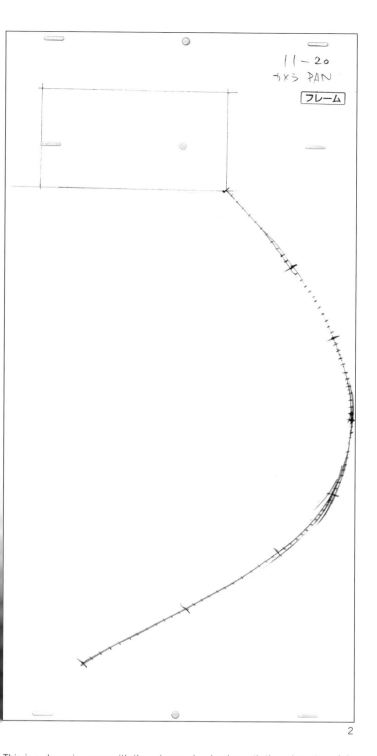

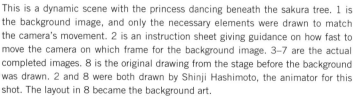

2

3

4

5

6

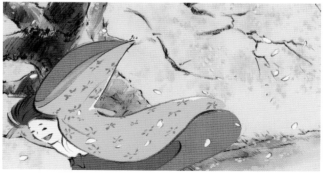

7

This is a dynamic scene with the princess dancing beneath the sakura tree. 1 is the background image, and only the necessary elements were drawn to match the camera's movement. 2 is an instruction sheet giving guidance on how fast to move the camera on which frame for the background image. 3–7 are the actual completed images. 8 is the original drawing from the stage before the background was drawn. 2 and 8 were both drawn by Shinji Hashimoto, the animator for this shot. The layout in 8 became the background art.

"We didn't do anything too complicated for this sequence. We just moved the camera as instructed and recreated the planned vision of animation. The animator for this scene was Shinji Hashimoto, and he often surprised me with his scene designs. It's not in this sequence, but he'd noted the individual steps for the camera work. I thought the movement was too straight, so I added some movement pulling to the side, and Hashimoto asked me to please follow the steps precisely since he had actually added movement so that it would shake slightly. When I did exactly that, I was impressed that we really got that effect."

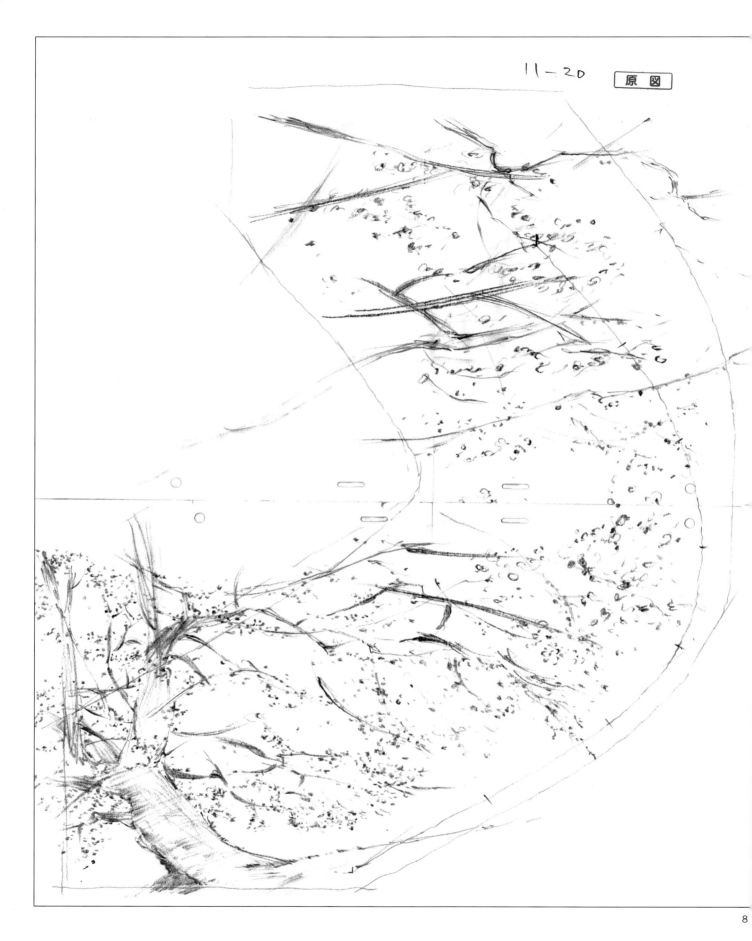

11-20 原図

"The sakura petals and the princess are dancing together in this one sequence. Then the wind changes in the middle of the sequence, so the petals go in the opposite direction, which gives rise to a really interesting effect. This was also not photography's work, it was all thanks to Hashimoto's animation."

Cinematic Expression 7
Swaying flowers and bee

[S11-C4 key animation/Shinji Hashimoto, background/Katsu Hisamura]

1

5

2

6

3

The flower up front sways and the bee on it flies off. It looks as though the background image is moving, but this flower was actually animated again based on the background elements. It was made to move in photography, staying close to the background look. 1–4 are the reference elements drawn by the art staff. 1–3 have only the flower parts drawn on transparent cels. 4 is the background grass drawn most faintly. 5–6 are the actual completed images. You almost can't tell the difference between the flowers created in animation and photography and the art elements.

"We also created this by layering paint outlines and texture animations over a principal line drawing. But with just that, it felt heavy, so we added different kinds of irregularities, a little blurriness and bleed, and slowly we got closer to the background that Oga drew. I think if you look really closely, you can tell the difference between the cel elements and the background, but the task this time was to try and make it as hard to tell as possible."

4

Cinematic Expression 8
Dragon cloud
[S13C-C11 key animation/Hiroyuki Morita, Tatsuzo Nishita, background/Kazuo Oga]

Background elements

Completed images

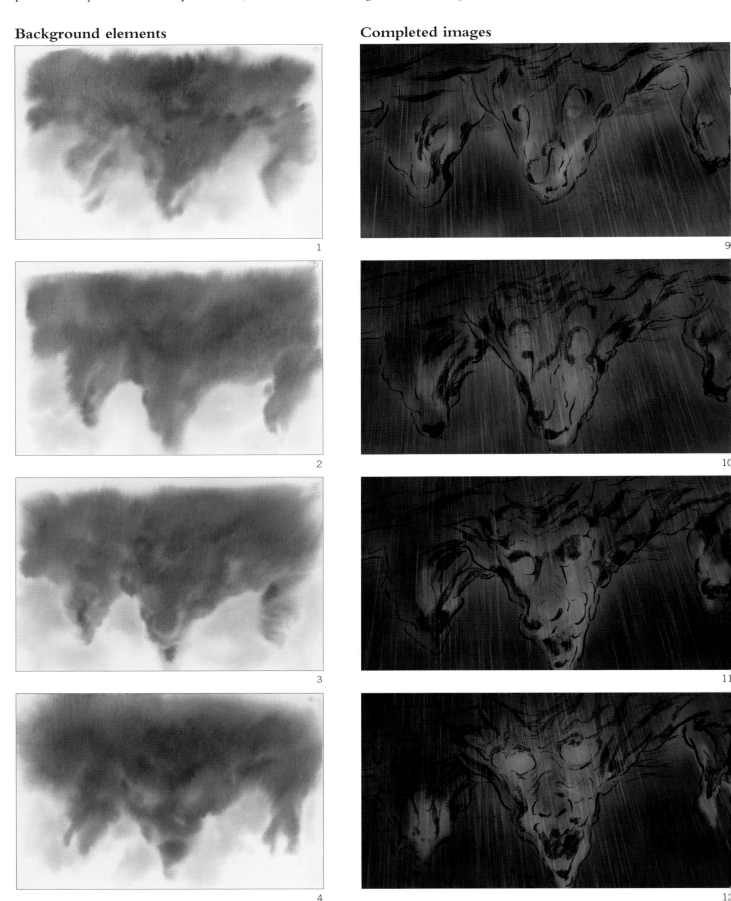

1

2

3

4

9

10

11

12

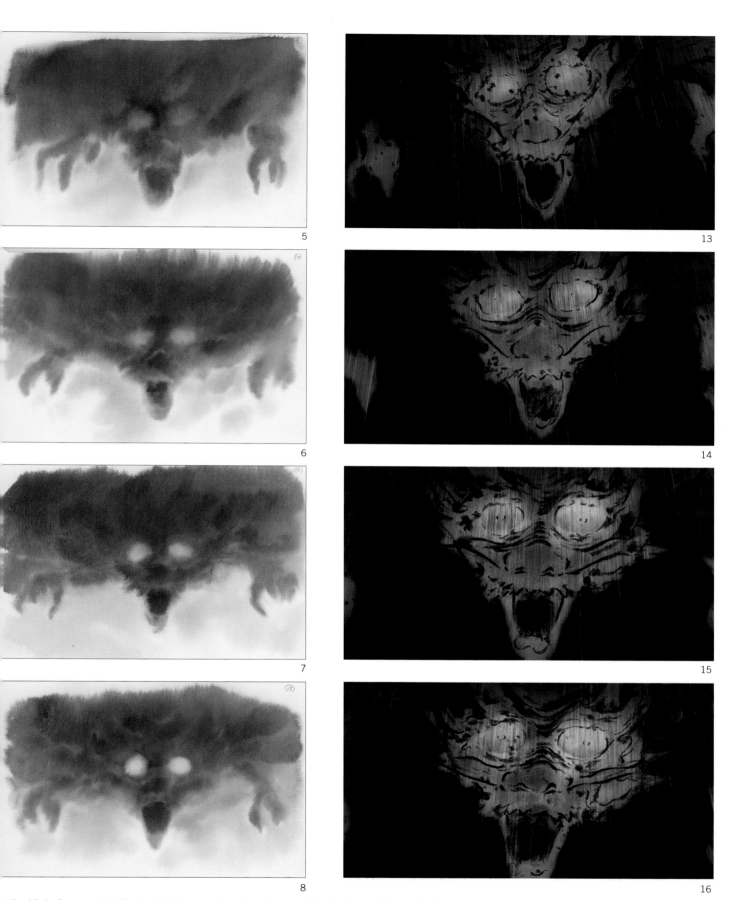

5

13

6

14

7

15

8

16

In the blink of an eye, the black cloud changes shape, transforming into the claws and torso of a dragon. This sequence was produced through a combination of animation and art. 1–8 are the changing cloud elements drawn by Kazuo Oga. 9–16 are the actual completed images.

"The shape of the dragon was drawn in animation, and the variation of the cloud inside it was created based on drawings by Oga. We processed the many pages they drew for us in pursuit of movement. The variation in the cloud is essentially all as it was in the original art, but we made it so that the lights and darks of the image were emphasized and tried to give a sense of greater depth and enormity. We also overlaid several images and did an overlap to produce the sense of gradual change, making it so that there's no discrepancy between the animation lines and the art inside them."

Cinematic Expression 9
Bamboo forest moving in the wind
[S1-C72 key animation/Akiko Yamaguchi, background/Kazuo Oga]

1

2

3

4

5

6

7

The depiction of the bamboo forest moving in the wind gives the impression that the background and itself is moving. 1–3 are the art board drawn by Kazuo Oga. 4 is the texture element for variation in the bamboo leaves drawn by Oga for the animation. 5 is bamboo made in photography based on the animation parts. 6–7 add variation to and copy this bamboo, placing them deftly all around the scene.

"We got the element with lots of green variation from Oga (4) and the animation elements with leaves flying, and finished this by increasing the number of them, changing the color, and changing the individual timing of their movement. This is one of the shots that took the most work in photography."

226

Cinematic Expression 10
Shadow of the moon king

[S17–C19 key animation/Tatsuzo Nishita, Atsushi Tamura, background/Kazuo Oga]

1

4

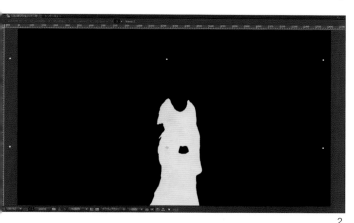

2

5

3

6

There is just the faintest of patterns in the cloud the people of the moon ride and the shadow of the moon king himself, and this moves slowly. 1 is the background element Kazuo Oga drew. 2 is the mask element for the moon king's shadow that is layered on 1. 3 fuses 2 and the actual animation elements. 4–7 are completed images. It's a bit hard to tell at this size, but the pattern on the moon king's shadow changes slightly.

"There's a faint pattern in the cloud and the moon king's shadow, and this moves bit by bit, something that was done because of an instruction from Takahata. The change is really such that if you don't look closely, you can't see it. The director said that it would be good in that way. I think it gives rise to a mysteriousness for the moon king and pulls the image together."

7

Cinematic Expression 11
The flight of the princess and Sutemaru

[S16C–C19 key animation/Shinji Hashimoto, background/Kazuo Oga, Yohei Takamatsu]

Imageboard by Yoshiyuki Momose

Scene 16 is the flight of the princess and Sutemaru. Working as the specially appointed scene designer, Yoshiyuki Momose did everything from design to storyboard, planning it together with Takahata. He also created a number of rough storyboards based on imagined scenes. Momose had previously done storyboards and layouts for other Takahata films, and as he did for *My Neighbors the Yamadas*, he handled an entire sequence himself here. In the initial plan, this was imagined as a scene where the princess and Sutemaru took in the business of living and dying of people in regions around the world as they flew. Momose created a number of pieces of imageboard for this. But in the end, the direction was changed to depict the heartfelt bonds of the princess and Sutemaru. Shown here are just some of the concept-art images Momose did. He also handled the final scene 17. Together with Takahata, he planned it until the envoy from the moon comes and returns home with the princess.

228

Art boards by Kazuo Oga

The two pieces above are art board drawn by Kazuo Oga for the flight scene with the princess and Sutemaru.
The scene with them flying through the ravine stayed in the storyboard until the final stages, but it was cut in
the end and all that was produced were these two images.

Expression of flight through CG

For the scene with the princess and Sutemaru flying, CG was used in this sequence and a few others, finished by the CG artist Tomoya Nakajima. The CG elements using background elements in 1–4 were fused with the animated characters in photography, and images as in 5–9 were created.

"This sequence, including the camerawork, was done by CG artist Nakamura. Photography was just the final combined part. The trees in the forest drawn by the art staff were cut out one by one to make about ninety elements, and these were repositioned in a 3D space. He created the forest, carefully adjusting the height differences, and the density and color balance of the trees. The sense of escape the instant the forest drops away and the ocean comes into view and the speed at which the camera moves up as if chasing the pair gave Nakajima and Takahata a lot of trouble."

6

5

2

1

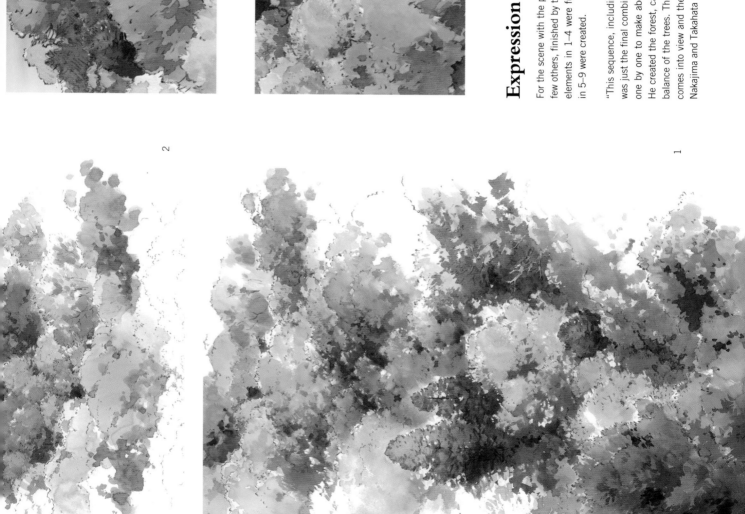

"Inochi no Kioku"
(When I Remember This Life)

Lyrics, Music and Performed by Kazumi Nikaido

The joy I felt when I touched you
Went deep, deep down
And seeped into
Every nook and cranny of this body

Even if I'm far away
And no longer understand anything
Even when the time comes
For this life to end

Everything of now
is everything of the past
We'll meet again, I'm sure
in some nostalgic place

The warmth you gave me
Deep, deep down
Comes to me now, complete
From a time long past

Steadily in my heart
The flames of passion give light
And softly soothe my pain
Down to the depths of my grief

Everything now
Is hope for the future
I'll remember, I'm sure
In some nostalgic place

Everything of now
is everything of the past
We'll meet again, I'm sure
In some nostalgic place

Everything now
Is hope for the future
I'll remember, I'm sure
When I remember this life

"Warabe Uta"
(Nursery Rhyme)
Lyrics by Isao Takahata and Riko Sakaguchi
Music by Isao Takahata

Round, round, go round,
Waterwheel, go round
Go round, and call Mr. Sun
Go round, and call Mr. Sun
Birds, bugs, beasts, grass, trees, flowers
Bring spring and summer, fall and winter
Bring spring and summer, fall and winter

Round, round, go round,
Waterwheel, go round
Go round, and call Mr. Sun
Go round, and call Mr. Sun
Birds, bugs, beasts, grass, trees, flowers
Flower, bear fruit, and die
Be born, grow up, and die
Still the wind blows. The rain falls
The waterwheel goes round
Lifetimes come and go in turn
Lifetimes come and go in turn

"Tennyo no Uta"
(Song of the Heavenly Maiden)
Lyrics by Isao Takahata and Riko Sakaguchi
Music by Isao Takahata

Go round, come round, come round,
O distant time
Come round, call back my heart
Come round, call back my heart
Birds, bugs, beasts, grass, trees, flowers
Teach me how to feel
If I hear that you pine for me, I will
return to you

[S11-C22 background/Kazuo Oga]

CREDITS

VOICES
Aki Asakura

Kengo Kora

Takeo Chii

Nobuko Miyamoto

Atsuko Takahata

Tomoko Tabata

Shinosuke Tatekawa

Takaya Kamikawa

Hikaru Ijuin

Ryudo Uzaki

Shichinosuke Nakamura

Isao Hashizume

Mirai Uchida	Fubomichi Takazawa
Reigo Mizoguchi	Hidenosuke Kawashiro
Minoru Matsumoto	Akio Nakadai
Ippei Sasaki	Kagetora Miura
Satsuki Okumori	Akari Iijima
Ai Uchida	Juria Takayanagi
Anju Takayanagi	Emi Tanaka
Shogo Hirama	Ryoto Ozeki
Kenji Yamauchi	Teruyuki Ishii
Tomohiko Kumagai	Hayato Kanno
Erika Osanai	Mina Hiroe
Michié	Makishi Suzu
Kyosuke Tachibana	Tomohiro Ogawa
Takayuki Seki	Kazuki Abe
Masatoshi Suzumoto	Tatsuya Yamamoto
Shinsuke Kishi	Hiroyuki Yamamoto
Takeshi Yoshimoto	Kohei Yada
Mikako Oshima	Tamaki Kojo

Yuji Miyake (Special Appearance)

Yukiji Asaoka (Cameo Appearance)

Tatsuya Nakadai

Production Staff
EXECUTIVE PRODUCER
Seiichiro Ujiie

DEPUTY EXECUTIVE PRODUCER
Yoshio Okubo

PLANNING
Toshio Suzuki

BASED ON THE JAPANESE FOLKTALE
"THE TALE OF THE BAMBOO CUTTER"

ORIGINAL CONCEPT
Isao Takahata

SCREENPLAY
Isao Takahata   Riko Sakaguchi

MUSIC
Joe Hisaishi

THEME SONG
"Inochi no Kioku" (When I Remember This Life)
Lyrics, Music and Performed by Kazumi Nikaido

SONGS
"Warabe Uta" (Nursery Rhyme)
"Tennyo no Uta" (Song of the Heavenly Maiden)
Lyrics by Isao Takahata and Riko Sakaguchi
Music by Isao Takahata

CHARACTER DESIGN
DIRECTING ANIMATOR
Osamu Tanabe

ART DIRECTOR
Kazuo Oga

SUPERVISING ANIMATOR
Kenichi Konishi

KEY ANIMATION
Shinji Hashimoto

Takayuki Hamada

Masashi Ando

Akiko Yamaguchi

KEY ANIMATION

Shunsuke Hirota	Ayako Hata
Shoko Nishigaki	Tatsuzo Nishita
Miwa Sasaki	Toshio Kawaguchi
Shogo Furuya	Atsushi Tamura
Ei Inoue	Emi Ageishi
Yoshihiro Osugi	Kuniyuki Ishii
Kazutaka Ozaki	Kumiko Kawana
Shimpei Kamata	Shigeo Akahori
Shigeru Kimishima	Yosuke Jimbo
Masako Sato	Tomomi Kamiya
Chiyomi Tsukamoto	Takashi Kawaguchi
Mami Sodeyama	Ayano Yagi
Takuya Saito	Kaori Hayashi
Tomoko Tani	Yuka Matsumura
Daizen Komatsuda	Takayuki Gotan
Hiroyuki Morita	Megumi Kagawa
Hideki Hamasu	Shinji Otsuka

PAINT OUTLINE AND TEXTURE ANIMATION
Masaya Saito

ANIMATION CHECK

Maiko Nogami	Emi Nakano
Yuka Saito	Emi Matsunaga

IN-BETWEEN ANIMATION

Ryosuke Mizuno	Yohei Nakano
Takuya Wada	Kanako Sekii
Reiko Mano	Moe Tanaka
Mitsunori Murata	Kaoru Hokiyama
Yuki Sato	Yoko Tanaka
Ryosuke Murahashi	Shiori Hosaka
Yukie Yamamoto	Masashi Omura
Soonha Hwang	Migyeong An
Younghee Park	Kumiko Tanihira
Yukari Yamaura	Mai Nakazato
Masami Nakanishi	Masakiyo Koyama
Akane Otani	Ayaka Saito
Yukari Furiya	Shin Oba
Aya Takahashi	Kokoro Takemoto
Ayano Okitsu	Ho Chan Won

Hisako Yaji	Takeshi Okoshi
Tomoyuki Kojima	Mika Matsumura
Yoshie Endo	Yu Horie
Rika Chijiiwa	Michiko Miyamoto
Tomomi Hamada	Nina Somekawa
Ai Takashi	Yu Yagi
Nozomi Kawashige	Yuki Kamiya
Naho Sekine	Tamami Izawa
Nobu Kakihira	Masaru Goto
Kumiko Terada	Kaori Ito
Yu Okuwaki	Rie Eyama
Setsuya Tanabe	Hiroko Tetsuka
Yukie Kaneko	Maiko Matsumura
Tomoko Miyata	Yukiko Muroga
Sumie Nishido	Hinako Goto
Yoonji Kim	Seiko Azuma
Mamiko Okada	Mariko Yoshida
Makoto Ohara	Megumi Matsumoto
Michiko Oda	Tsubomi Ishihara
Azusa Fujita	Azusa Sakuma
Satoko Shimoji	Chie Nagano
Mizuho Fukuda	Rie Horinouchi
Kaoru Yanagisawa	Sairi Ogawa
Haruna Hashimoto	Yuka Hirata
Hitomi Shiroki	Takana Shirai
Etsuko Tamakoshi	Hitomi Tateno
Kaori Fujii	Masako Akita
Misa Koyasu	Emi Tamura
Shoko Nagasawa	Shiori Fujisawa
Yui Matsuura	Asako Matsumura
Naoya Wada	Miki Ito
Yuko Tagawa	

PAINT OUTLINE ANIMATION CHECK
Noriko Akiyama

PAINT OUTLINE ANIMATION

Yoriko Mochizuki	Yasumi Tanaka
Yayoi Toki	Akiko Kumada
Yuka Aono	Maiko Ochiai
Saki Saegusa	Akiko Taniguchi
Shuji Maruyama	Kenichi Otomo
Yosuke Okuda	Miho Namekawa
Akemi Ueda	Hiroko Kando
Ai Kaneko	Risa Ogasawara
Masato Ujibe	Shuhei Fukuda
Sae Akama	Takahiro Okawa
Makoto Yaguchi	Dai Misawa
Hiroyuki Moriguchi	Shota Sugimoto
Asami Yamaguchi	Yasuo Ishii
Momoko Tamakoshi	Konomi Sato
Yuka Fujii	Kota Shimamura
Yu Okagaki	Takahiro Inoue
Kosuke Kobashi	Akiko Oshima
Kayo Sakazume	Shiomi Yamada
Megumi Tonegawa	Akane Okuchi
Saori Hagita	Akari Takagaki
Miyu Nagata	Anri Yamazaki
Yuki Sato	Kaoru Higashidani
Fumi Saraie	Kazuto Wakayama
Kenzo Yamazaki	Hiromi Niwa
Megumi Hirota	Takashi Kano
Satoshi Semba	Ryota Usui
Yuri Yagisawa	Yoshimi Shizuka
Nanako Egami	Yuichi Tajima
Kazunari Araki	Kenji Taketani
Wenlung Hsu	Ritsuko Taniguchi
Masaru Okuma	Teppei Okuda
Junya Sato	Fumiki Yamada
Satsuki Muramatsu	Yukie Watanabe
Eiji Yamamori	Rie Nakagome

Masayo Ando
Alexandra Weihrauch
Makiko Suzuki
Asami Ishikado
Emi Ota
Yasumi Ogura
Sachiko Kunitake
Yoshie Noguchi
Mitsuki Chiba
Ryosuke Tsuchiya

Akiko Teshima
Mariko Matsuo
Shinichiro Yamada
Yui Osaki
Akiyo Okuda
Naoko Kawahara
Tomoyo Nishita
Misaki Kikuta
Yeefeng Chan
Yuka Matsumura

SUPPORTING ANIMATION STUDIOS

Anime Torotoro
Oh - Production
Kyushu Animation
Studio Cockpit
Studio Takuranke
David Production
Nakamura Production
Studio Pierrot
Vega Entertainment
MAGIC BUS
Yuhodo
Wafu Animation
C2C
Production I.G
Wish

The Answerstudio
Ozawa Design Works
CONNECT
Studio Comet
Tatsunoko Production
Doga Kobo
Nippon Animation
Project Team Sarah
Bones
Madhouse
Lidenfilms Osaka Studio
A.P.P.P.
MAA MOPICS
STUDIO4°C

BACKGROUNDS

Tomotaka Kubo
Ayumi Kugawa
Yohei Takamatsu
Tatsuya Kushida
Satoko Nakamura

Takashi Kurahashi
Katsu Hisamura
Yumi Hosaka
Shiho Sato

COLOR SETTING

Yukiko Kakita

DIGITAL INK AND PAINT CHECK

Fumie Kawamata

Kumi Nanjo

DIGITAL INK AND PAINT

Yui Ito
Yoshimi Shibata
Natsuko Inohara
Ritsuki Miyamoto
Sanae Seno

Akiko Shimizu
Natsumi Watanabe
Yuina Iizuka
Michiko Saito

Hisako Sasaki
Emiko Okui
Yoko Chiba
Taiki Egusa
Maki Omoto
Yukari Kuno
Yoko Wakabayashi
Akemi Kato
Miki Kobayashi
Yoshimi Hashizume
Katsuhiko Shiroto
Terumi Narita
Kaori Kamata
Yohei Nishiwaki
Yusaku Harada
Erina Yamamoto
Hitomi Kashihara
Miyuki Akamatsu
Miyu Toyoshima
Yoichi Senzui
Atsushi Tamura
Norihiko Miyoshi
Keiko Itogawa

Atsuko Ito
Naoko Sunahara
Rieko Umemura
Hitomi Yamase
Kanako Tajiri
Yumi Fujiwara
Junko Takeuchi
Rie Kitazawa
Satomi Hatano
Shinami Yoshikawa
Tomoko Toki
Midori Saito
Takashi Saito
Eri Yoshiki
Maki Yamamoto
Yukari Hashimoto
Sonoe Yoshida
Ayako Kitamura
Kumiko Mizoguchi
Junji Yabuta
Hidenori Shibahara
Miki Umezawa
Masafumi Inoue

Shun Iwasawa
Takeshi Nakamura
Hiromi Takahashi
Kanako Takayanagi
Naomi Mori
Hiroaki Ishii
Yuki Komatsu
Misato Aita
Atsushi Okui

Junya Saito
Tomoya Shinmi
Kazuko Karube
Yukie Tamura
Rie Kojo
Eiko Matsushima
Nana Takei
Yuki Kashima

SUPPORTING DIGITAL INK AND PAINT STUDIOS

Wish
Igel-Nest
Studio Gimlet

Animation Time
Anitus-Kobe

DIRECTOR OF DIGITAL IMAGING

Keisuke Nakamura

DIGITAL CAMERA AND COMPOSITE OPERATORS

Yukiko Kaga
Tomoyuki Shiokawa
Kazumasa Someya
Yusuke Okamoto
Kotaro Beppu

Yuma Akasu
Rumi Ishiguro
Koji Takahashi
Hisashi Akimoto

BACKGROUND SCANNING

Takeshi Ogawa

Miho Kawanishi

SUPPORTING STUDIO FOR ANIMATION SCANNING

Assez Finaud Fabric.
Atsuko Okui
Yoshiaki Kayaba
Megumi Tanaka
Haruka Ito
Atsuko Shibata

Kanae Ouchi
Rieko Koike
Shoko Fujimaki
Tasuku Takagi
Yasunao Kondo

SPECIALLY APPOINTED SCENE PLANNER

Yoshiyuki Momose

COMPUTER GRAPHICS

Tomonari Nakajima

ASSISTANT STORYBOARDS ARTISTS

Masako Sato
Shinji Hashimoto

Shinsaku Sasaki

SOUND DESIGNER

Naoko Asari

DIALOGUE RECORDING ENGINEER

Akihiko Ono

SOUND RE-RECORDING MIXER

Koji Kasamatsu

SOUND EFFECTS

Tomoko Otsuka

ASSISTANT DIALOGUE RECORDING ENGINEERS

Hajime Takagi
Shuji Suzuki

Miki Nomura
Tsukasa Yokoyama

FOLEY ARTISTS

Akihiko Okase

Mizuki Ito

FOLEY EDITOR

Natsuko Inoue

TECHNICAL SUPPORT

Naoto Takeshima

VIDEO PLAYBACK OPERATOR

Hideho Kikuchi

Shinichiro Koshi

STUDIO COORDINATORS

Sadaaki Nishinoo
Osamu Murata

Chiaki Tachikawa

CASTING

Queen's Promotion
Keiko Ogata
Hazuki Yamamura

Kaori Sakai

SOUND PRODUCTION SUPPORT

Toho Studios
Toho Studios Post-Production Center
Edo-Tokyo Open Air Architectural Museum

Toho Studio Service
Tokyo T.V. Center

CONDUCTOR, PIANO

Joe Hisaishi

MUSIC PERFORMED BY

Tokyo Symphony Orchestra

GU ZHENG

Xiao-Qing Jiang

MUSIC RECORDING ENGINEER

Suminobu Hamada

MUSIC RECORDED AT

Muza Kawasaki Symphony Hall
Bunkamura Studio

MUSIC PRODUCTION

Wonder City
Maki Fujisawa
Akiko Suzawa

Yasuhiro Maeda

CLASSICAL COURT MUSIC

"Uho Bairo Hyojochoshi", "Hakuchu"

TITLES

Malin Post

EDITING

Toshihiko Kojima

PRODUCTION MANAGER

Toshio Yoshikawa

ASSISTANTS TO THE DIRECTOR

Akiko Matsuo

Yuichiro Kido

PRODUCTION ASSISTANTS

Kazuyuki Shimada
Satoko Okubo
Kenji Imura

Akihiko Suzuki
Chihiro Okada
Aya Hashimoto

POST PRODUCTION

Tamaki Kojo

PRODUCTION SECRETARIES

Kanako Aoki

Mine Shibuya

PRODUCTION MANAGEMENT

Shinsuke Nonaka

PRODUCTION ADMINISTRATION

Taisei Ishiseko
Daisuke Nishikata
Minako Nagasawa

Toshiyuki Kawabata
Tetsu Shinagawa
Yoichiro Kugimiya

PRODUCER'S OFFICE
Nobuko Shiraki
Yoko Ihira
Chiaki Okuda
Chieko Tamura
Shuhei Tadano

PRODUCER IN TRAINING
Nobuo Kawakami

PUBLIC RELATIONS
Shin Hashida
Nozomu Ito
Chihiro Tsukue
Mayu Naito
Setsuko Kurihara
Yumiko Nishimura
Kazumi Kobayashi

MERCHANDISING DEVELOPMENT
Tomomi Imai
Mika Yasuda
Koichi Asano
Naomi Atsuta

PUBLISHING MANAGER
Yukari Tai

PUBLISHING
Hisanori Nukada
Kyoko Hirabayashi
Kyoko Konishi
Chikashi Saito
Yuri Morita
Satoko Kitazawa

SPECIAL EVENTS
Kazuyoshi Tanaka
Ryoko Tsutsui
Takayuki Aoki
Kan Miyoshi
Kenzo Ochiai
Noriko Takami

PERSONNEL MANAGER
Yuichiro Mochizuki

STUDIO ADMINISTRATION
Miyuki Shimamiya
Satomi Sasaki
Hiroyuki Saito
Natsuki Ebisawa
Saori Uchida
Tokuko Sato
Tomomi Hagihara
Hikari Hayama
Kiyoko Tsuge
Shunichi Iwasaki
Hisayo Ito
Tamami Yamamoto
Yukiko Miyasaka
Miyuki Ishii
Yuko Nomura
Masahiro Suzuki
Maho Honobe
Sueko Numazawa
Keiko Kido
Tsuneo Sawai

FINANCE MANAGER
Noriyoshi Tamagawa

ACCOUNTING
Takayasu Ito
Satoshi Otsuka
Junko Ito
Akio Ichimura
Hiromi Ito

CORPORATE DEVELOPMENT
Kazumi Inaki

SYSTEM MANAGEMENT
Noriyuki Kitakawachi
Shoji Makihara
Yugo Hayashi

OVERSEAS PROMOTION MANAGERS
Geoffrey Wexler
Mikiko Takeda

OVERSEAS PROMOTION
Nao Amisaki
Noriko Tsushi
Evan Ma
Satoko Takano

AUDITOR
Hirotaka Nakao

SPECIAL THANKS TO
Yume Arikawa
Fumiko Isomae
Miyuki Ito
Toshio Otake
Tomoko Okada
Wataru Kakubari
Koichi Katsushima
Daisaku Kawase
Hiroki Kikuno
Kana Kimura
Takeyasu Koganezawa
Shinji Goto
Shiroyuki Kon
Yoshichika Sakamoto
Miho Sata
Yuki Sato
Masahiro Shinoki
Akinori Shudo
Seiichiro Sekine
Toshiyuki Takahashi
Yohei Taneda
Yoko Terakoshi
Satoshi Nakano
Yasuhisa Harada
Haruna Hirose
Atsushi Fukushi
Tadahiro Hoshi
Tamako Matsutoya
Hiroshi Miyashita
Naoya Moritani
Manaho Mori
Keizo Yoshikawa
Katsuhiko Yoshida
Tomoe Iijima
Hidenori Ito
Kohei Ueno
Yoshito Oyama
Ryutaro Ozawa
Yoshiichiro Kashiwagi
Hiroshi Kadowaki
Osamu Kawada
Seigo Kimata
Naho Kimura
Ai Kodama
Hideaki Kobayashi
Nobue Saito
Yoshiki Sakurai
Toshikazu Sato
Taketoshi Sado
Shigeki Shimizu
Yasuhiro Suzuki
Tadashi Setomitsu
Hideo Tanaka
Eri Tamura
Michiko Nagai
Yoshiyuki Hatori
Takahiro Hirao
Tomomi Fukao
Bryan Whitehead
Satoshi Matsushita
Saki Miyaoku
Takuo Murase
Masaki Morita
Maiko Yahata
Tsuyoshi Yoshikawa
Kenichi Yoda
Center for Ethnological Visual Documentation

PROMOTIONAL SPONSOR
KDDI
EYEFUL HOME

SPECIAL MEDIA SUPPORT
Lawson
The Yomiuri Shimbun

ADVERTISING PRODUCERS
Akito Takahashi
Tomoko Hosokawa

ADVERTISING
Kenichi Arao
Rieko Matsuki
Yukio Shinohara
Kazue Tsukagoshi
Masaru Yabe
Mieko Hara
Hiroyuki Orihara
Hajime Murata
Shoichiro Saito
Saori Ueda
Yukari Nishikawa
Genji Sakai
Yukari Nomura
Michiyo Koyanagi
Hiroshi Yajima
Aya Maruyama
Aki Tsutagawa
Fumino Watanabe

FILM TRAILERS PRODUCTION
Keiichi Itagaki

THE TALE OF THE PRINCESS KAGUYA PRODUCTION COMMITTEE
Nippon Television Network
Kimio Maruyama
Daisuke Kadoya
Toshikazu Mori
Naoto Hatakeyama
Tomoko Jo
Hiroko Miyazaki
Naoki Iwasa
Mayumi Hirakata

Dentsu
Tadashi Ishii
Toshihiro Yamamoto
Shuichi Machida
Yoshio Takada
Yutaka Ishikawa
Ryuichi Ikeda

Akitoshi Maeda
Misato Kamei
Satoshi Suzuki

Hakuhodo DY Media Partners
Hisao Omori
Yoshikuni Murata
Toshihiro Komatsu
Masato Tachibana
Akio Kobayashi
Michio Yamamoto
Madoka Hosoya

Walt Disney Japan
Paul Candland
Masami Takahashi
Yuko Muranaka
Hidetaka Kokubu
Takayuki Tsukagoshi
Koji Kishimoto
Yukio Yamashita
Ayako Dan

d-rights
Daizo Suzuki
Toshiya Takasaki
Kino Arai
Toru Itabashi
Kota Sugiyama
Asako Hio

Toho
Hideyuki Takai
Satoshi Chida
Shimpei Ise
Hikaru Onoda
Yoshishige Shimatani
Minami Ichikawa
Taichi Ueda

KDDI
Makoto Takahashi
Takashi Suga
Masako Yano
Jun Okabe
Takahiro Kishi
Toshitake Amamiya
Koichi Kawakami
Shingo Niori
San Kim
Takahiro Hirato

ASSOCIATE PRODUCERS
Seiji Okuda
Ryoichi Fukuyama
Naoya Fujimaki

DIGITAL LAB
IMAGICA
DATA CONFORM
DATA MANAGEMENT

COLOR MANAGEMENT

DIGITAL CINEMA MASTERING

LAB COORDINATION
LAB MANAGEMENT
Naoto Hosonuma
Sho Ogoshi
Daijiro Adachi
Toshiki Yura
Wataru Matsumoto
Miho Sugiyama
Mizue Yamada
Yuriko Sato
Kazunori Nagasawa

PRODUCTION SUPPORT
T2studio / Kentaro Takahashi

PRODUCTION
Koji Hoshino
Studio Ghibli

PRODUCER
Yoshiaki Nishimura

DIRECTED BY
Isao Takahata

First poster released.

かぐや姫の物語

姫の犯した罪と罰。

高畑勲監督作品

朝倉あき

高良健吾　地井武男　宮本信子　高畑淳子　田畑智子　立川志の輔　上川隆也　伊集院光　宇崎竜童　中村七之助　橋爪功　朝丘雪路（特別出演）　仲代達矢

製作／氏家齊一郎 ●原作／「竹取物語」 ●原案・脚本・監督／高畑勲 ●脚本／坂口理子 ●音楽／久石譲（ワンダーシティ・アソシエイツ）●主題歌／「いのちの記憶」二階堂和美（スピードスターレコーズ）●スタジオジブリ・日本テレビ・電通・博報堂DYMP・ディズニー・三菱商事・東宝・KDDI 提携作品 ●特別協賛／KDDI・アイフルホーム ●特別協力／ローソン・読売新聞 ●配給／東宝

11月23日㈷全国ロードショー

kaguyahime-monogatari.jp

Third poster released.

THE ART OF

THE TALE OF
THE PRINCESS KAGUYA

Based on the Studio Ghibli Film
Original Concept and
Screenplay Written and Directed by

Isao Takahata

English Adaptation/Jocelyne Allen
Design & Layout /Yukiko Whitley
Editor/Masumi Washington

Kaguya-hime no Monogatari
(The Tale of The Princess Kaguya)
Copyright © 2013 Hatake Jimusho - Studio Ghibli – NDHDMTK
All rights reserved.

© 2014 Studio Ghibli
First published in Japan by Studio Ghibli Inc.

Printed in China

Published by VIZ Media, LLC P.O. Box 77010
San Francisco, CA 94103

10 9 8 7 6 5 4 3 2 1

First Printing, April 2022